Gary Williams, PhD

Handbook fo.
Learning in `

Pre-publication
REVIEWS,
COMMENTARIES,
EVALUATIONS . . .

"**H**ere is a book written in plain English, simple to read and understand, that covers all the basic questions that should be asked by institution and lecturer alike before embarking on distance education flexible learning materials. What is flexible learning, who should be involved, how development teams should be created, what should be produced, how it should be delivered, how it should be written, and how it will be used are all covered. This is essential reading for anyone thinking of starting such a venture."

Stephen J. Craig-Smith, BSc (Hons), MEd, MSc, PhD
Deputy Head and Program Director, School of Tourism and Leisure Management, University of Queensland, Australia

"**T**his text provides a sound framework for the development of distance learning programs using both print- and Internet-based approaches. Rather than just a treatise on the theoretical basis for the arguments in support of distance learning, the author provides practical advice to assist those interested in challenging and changing their approaches to teaching.

Chapters such as that dealing with project management issues help to ensure that readers develop skills that are critical for the success of their distance learning projects. Other chapters logically link the educational design steps that are necessary for ensuring the success of the project. Although the case studies have a tourism focus, this text will be a valuable resource for those involved in teaching across a range of other disciplines."

Bill Lord, BHlthSc, MEd
Senior Lecturer, Monash University, Melbourne, Australia

More pre-publication
REVIEWS, COMMENTARIES, EVALUATIONS . . .

"This is an important book for a variety of audiences! As a resource for educational designers (and their managers) in particular, it is invaluable. The book is easy to read and is full of practical information that can be logically applied in the design and development of flexible learning resources.

Pedagogically and philosophically appealing, the text focuses on learning and teaching being supported, but not driven, by multimedia. Teachers, students, and learning resource developers all share the focus to create a balanced perspective of a flexible learning environment. The information and ideas provided in this unique handbook are not only applicable to the distance education mode of delivery but equally to all modes of delivery."

Louise Berg, MA, DipEd
Lecturer in Education,
Charles Sturt University,
Australia

"This book walks you through each stage of developing distance learning materials. Thanks to numerous examples, the instructions are easily understood.

Each chapter can be used as a stand-alone module to review, develop, and/or manage teaching materials. I would use this book as a reference guide if asked to manage or start a project, develop resources, create a Web site, or manage courses in the distance as well as traditional teaching modes.

I plan to keep this book on my reference shelf within arm's reach."

Ben Dewald, EdD
Associate Professor,
The Collins School of Hospitality Management,
California State Polytechnic University,
Pomona

THHP   **THRP**

The Haworth Hospitality Press®
The Haworth Reference Press™
Imprints of The Haworth Press, Inc.
New York • London • Oxford

Handbook for Distance Learning in Tourism

Handbook for Distance Learning in Tourism

Gary Williams, PhD

The Haworth Hospitality Press®
The Haworth Reference Press™
Imprints of The Haworth Press, Inc.
New York • London • Oxford

For more information on this book or to order, visit
http://www.haworthpress.com/store/product.asp?sku=5346

or call 1-800-HAWORTH (800-429-6784) in the United States and Canada
or (607) 722-5857 outside the United States and Canada

or contact orders@HaworthPress.com

Published by

The Haworth Hospitality Press® and The Haworth Reference Press™, imprints of The Haworth
Press, Inc., 10 Alice Street, Binghamton, NY 13904-1580.

Cover design by Kerry E. Mack.

Library of Congress Cataloging-in-Publication Data

Williams, Gary, 1966-
    Handbook for distance learning in tourism / Gary Williams.
        p. cm.
    Includes bibliographical references and index.
    ISBN-13: 978-0-7890-1859-5 (hard : alk. paper)
    ISBN-10: 0-7890-1859-4 (hard : alk. paper)
    ISBN-13: 978-0-7890-1860-1 (pbk. : alk. paper)
    ISBN-10: 0-7890-1860-8 (pbk. : alk. paper)
    1. Tourism—Study and teaching (Higher) 2. University extension. I. Title.

G155.7.W56 2005
910'.71'1—dc22

                                                                    2004022092

CONTENTS

Preface   ix

Acknowledgments   xi

**Chapter 1. Introduction to Flexible Learning
and the Case Study**   1

Objectives   1
Topic 1.1: What Is a Flexible Learning Environment?   2
Topic 1.2: Maximizing the Return on Investment   4
Topic 1.3: Introducing the Case Study   7
Topic 1.4: The Development Model   11
Key Points   14

Chapter 2. The Project Manager   15

Objectives   15
Topic 2.1: Every Project Has a Manager   15
Topic 2.2: The Roles and Characteristics of a Project
   Manager   17
Topic 2.3: Project Management Aids   22
Topic 2.4: The Project As Organized Chaos   24
Key Points   26

Chapter 3. Starting a Project   27

Objectives   27
Topic 3.1: The Spark   28
Topic 3.2: Developing and Buying Resources   29
Topic 3.3: The Project Team   31
Topic 3.4: Stakeholder Meetings   37
Topic 3.5: Maximizing Project Ownership   44
Topic 3.6: Considerations Before Committing to a Project—
   A Self-Appraisal for Teachers   45
Key Points   51

Chapter 4. Educational and Design Foundations   53

Objectives   53
Topic 4.1: Introduction   54
Topic 4.2: Constructivism—A Theory of Knowledge   54

Topic 4.3: Ensuring Quality Content   59
Topic 4.4: Educational Design Guidelines for Learning
   Resources   65
Topic 4.5: Writing a Course Outline   73
Topic 4.6: Copyright   74
Key Points   81

Chapter 5. Media Foundations   83

Objectives   83
Topic 5.1: Introduction   84
Topic 5.2: The Teacher Is Essential   85
Topic 5.3: Determining the Needs, Wants, and Technology
   Access of Students   87
Topic 5.4: Secondary Determinants—Teacher, Institution,
   and Course Factors   90
Topic 5.5: Using Media Instead of a Medium   94
Key Points   96

Chapter 6. Developing Print Resources   97

Objectives   97
Topic 6.1: Introduction   98
Topic 6.2: Advantages and Disadvantages of Print
   Learning Resources   101
Topic 6.3: Production   104
Topic 6.4: Design   117
Topic 6.5: Maintenance and Revision   126
Key Points   128

Chapter 7. Developing and Using Web Sites   129

Objectives   129
Topic 7.1: Introduction   130
Topic 7.2: Advantages and Disadvantages of Web Sites   130
Topic 7.3: Using the World Wide Web   134
Topic 7.4: Production   135
Topic 7.5: Design   148
Topic 7.6: Maintenance and Revision   161
Key Points   163

Chapter 8. Computer-Mediated Contact   165

Objectives   165
Topic 8.1: Introduction   165

Topic 8.2: The Advantages and Challenges of Computer-
    Mediated Contact   167
Topic 8.3: Teachers' Roles   171
Topic 8.4: Training and Support Roles   181
Key Points   184

Chapter 9. Course Management Systems   185

Objectives   185
Topic 9.1: Introduction   186
Topic 9.2: The Advantages and Challenges of Course
    Management Systems   187
Topic 9.3: A Teacher's Perspective—Using a Course
    Management System   195
Topic 9.4: Training and Support Roles   197
Key Points   201

Chapter 10. Teaching in a Flexible Learning Environment   203

Objectives   203
Topic 10.1: Introduction   204
Topic 10.2: Before a Course Starts   205
Topic 10.3: The Start of a Course   207
Topic 10.4: During a Course   209
Topic 10.5: The Responsibilities of Educational Designers   214
Key Points   215

Chapter 11. Being a Student in a Flexible Learning Environment   217

Objectives   217
Topic 11.1: Introduction   218
Topic 11.2: The Advantages and Challenges of Flexible
    Learning   219
Topic 11.3: You Have Enrolled in a Flexible Learning
    Course—What Now?   224
Topic 11.4: Making the Most of Learning Resources   229
Key Points   234

References   235

Index   239

ABOUT THE AUTHOR

Gary Williams, PhD, is an educational technologist who has worked in the field of distance and flexible education for eight years. Dr. Williams has fulfilled many of the roles, including project manager, educational designer, and content writer, associated with the development of print-based and Internet-based learning and teaching resources. He also has expertise in staff development and Web site design and programming. His research interests and publications span the educational technology field, with a current focus on applications within the hospitality education sector. Dr. Williams received his PhD and BSc (First Hons) from The University of Western Australia.

Dr. Williams is currently an educational technology consultant based in Perth, Western Australia. A major client of Dr. Williams' is the School of Hotel and Tourism Management at The Hong Kong Polytechnic University, where previously as a Project Fellow he was responsible for the establishment of the school's flexible learning courses. Dr. Williams has also worked as a Senior Educational Designer at one of Australia's largest providers of distance learning courses. He was the lead editor of the book *The Internet and Travel and Tourism Education* (Haworth).

Preface

This handbook is about developing and using print-based and Internet-based flexible learning resources designed for courses in which students infrequently, if ever, attend on-campus classes. Such courses are a regular part of tourism education, in which working professionals and nontraditional students engage in continuous enhancement of their qualifications.

You may be a teacher wanting to use your existing course notes to develop a flexible learning package, a Web site, or both. You may be an educational designer or project manager working as part of a team developing resources. Or you may be a teacher wanting information about how to teach in a flexible environment. This handbook is written for such an audience.

The handbook is based on the following personal beliefs that have crystallized during my years of educational design and project management:

- Flexible learning projects in universities and colleges often involve people fulfilling a variety of roles. Although in theory a project involves a team of specialists, the reality is that often one person, or a few, fulfill all roles. For example, a teacher may be a one-person project team acting as the project manager, content writer, and educational designer.
- Teachers are essential as content writers and instructors. Sometimes there is a perception that in a flexible learning environment the teachers' roles are diminished compared to their roles in on-campus courses. I disagree. Teachers are crucial not only during the development of learning resources but also during the teaching of flexible learning courses.
- Project management of flexible learning projects is an art and a science. An "organized chaos" approach to management that recognizes the need for flexibility and adaptability can assist in producing quality learning resources.

• Many of the principles of teaching and learning that apply in on-campus courses also apply in flexible courses, as they are related environments. Therefore many of the resources and teaching and learning skills associated with flexible learning can also be useful in on-campus situations.

This book is based on reality and experience. My goal is to present practical and applied information in a descriptive and conversational style. Although the case studies will be of particular interest to tourism educators, the book aims to help people from all disciplines interested in developing resources and teaching in a flexible learning environment. For those wanting to go beyond this handbook, the Web site (garywilliams.iinet.net.au/flexiblelearning) contains details of resources arranged on a chapter-by-chapter basis.

Acknowledgments

Although this handbook has one author, without the support and suggestions of many people it would not have been written. In particular, I thank the following people.

For five years I have worked with Ms. Creamy Kong. In that time we have been involved in the development of flexible learning print-based packages, Web sites, and the implementation of an Internet-based course management system. She is also the creator of the handbook's cartoons. I thank her for her support, advice, and creativity throughout the years.

It has been a pleasure to work with and learn from many of the staff and students of the School of Hotel and Tourism Management, at The Hong Kong Polytechnic University. Professor Ray Pine and Professor Kaye Chon in particular provided the support essential to project success. Michele Webster was kind enough to critique the initial outline and offer suggestions. Finally, I thank Leslie for her continued support and encouragement, and helping me see the beauty in living as well as the satisfaction that comes from expressing one's thoughts to others.

Chapter 1

Introduction to Flexible Learning and the Case Study

Establishing a flexible learning environment involves integrating learning, teaching, and supporting resources so that students can select from a range of learning opportunities. This requires a significant commitment by an institution. To maximize the return on investment, the use of the resources by a variety of student groups, both on campus and off campus, should be considered.

In this chapter, the tourism education case study, which is the main source of examples and conceptual illustrations in this handbook, is introduced, and the related development model is outlined.

OBJECTIVES

1. To explain the definition of a flexible learning environment and the associated terminology used in the handbook
2. To recommend that flexible learning resources be used as core and supplementary materials in traditional on-campus environments, as well as in flexible learning environments
3. To provide an overview of the flexible learning project, which is the case study presented throughout this handbook
4. To outline a development model for flexible learning projects that involves the design, production, use, evaluation, maintenance, and revision of learning resources

TOPIC 1.1: WHAT IS A FLEXIBLE LEARNING ENVIRONMENT?

The terminology of flexible learning varies among practitioners. The goal of this topic is to make you aware of the meanings I use, thereby helping you to use this handbook.

A **student** *is someone developing an understanding of the world.*

A **teacher** *helps people develop their understandings of the world.*

For the purposes of this handbook, students are people enrolled in a program of study, consisting of a number of courses. Teachers can also be called academics, lecturers, and professors.

In a **flexible learning environment,** *three types of resources—learning, teaching, and supporting—are integrated so that students have some control over the learning resources they use, when they use them, and how they use them.*

A **learning resource** *is something that students use to help them develop their understandings of course content. It is a source of information.*

Examples of learning resources are teachers, fellow students, work colleagues, libraries, Web sites, printed notes, CD-ROMs, videos, television programs, newspapers, and textbooks.

A **teaching resource** *is something that teachers use to help them help students.*

A **supporting resource** *is something that both students and teachers utilize to facilitate the use of learning and teaching resources.*

Many learning resources are also teaching resources. For example, a teacher may base a tutorial on the notes to be given to students and a video. The notes and video are serving as both teaching and learning resources. Examples of items usually used only as teaching resources

include textbook instructor guides and manuals about using computer software to create and administer tests.

Supporting resources provide the infrastructure to aid learning and teaching processes. An administration office is an example of a supporting resource. Such an office

- manages assignment submissions and returns;
- coordinates the enrollment process; and
- serves as a contact point for students.

The meaning of the term *flexible learning* is itself flexible. The defining characteristic is choice.

A ***flexible learning project*** *results in the development of resources, through a process of design, production, use, evaluation, maintenance, and revision.*

Although this handbook focuses on providing choice for students, there are others for whom you may want to provide flexibility. You need to ask the following questions:

Who are you interested in providing choice for?
What types of choices do you want to provide?
How do you intend to provide them? (See Exhibit 1.1)

TOPIC 1.2: MAXIMIZING THE RETURN ON INVESTMENT

I believe it is important to have an awareness of one measure of success in particular—maximization of the return on investment—at the start of a project. This awareness can help you explain the benefits of the project and receive the support of colleagues.

The **return on investment** *is maximized when consideration has been given to making a resource available to teachers and students who are not part of the environment for which the resource is specifically designed.*

EXHIBIT 1.1. Language Makes a Difference

During the first two months of the HTM Project (Topic 1.3) in my role as project manager and educational designer I met with many people to explain the project and obtain their support. I used the terms *flexible learning* and *distance learning* interchangeably.

However, I realized that in the university, terms such as *distance learning* and *distance education* were viewed unfavorably. The reasons were complex. My perception was that many staff associated the word *distance* with providing second-class teaching that cost students money and staff their jobs.

I decided to describe the work only as a flexible learning project. You can argue that I should have attempted to correct the misconceptions about distance learning. However, a project manager must be pragmatic and prioritize. My priority was to get the project started with the necessary support of teachers and senior university management.

For example, you may develop learning resources as part of providing a flexible learning environment for students who work full-time in the tourism industry and want to upgrade their qualifications. The resources are designed to take into account the characteristics, needs, and wants of the students. This does not mean that only those students and their teachers should have access to the resources. In order to maximize the return on investment, they should be available for use by other teachers and students.

Consider the development of a 400-page strategic marketing package. The package is designed to support students who have to decide when to attend on-campus classes. That is, a flexible learning environment exists where the package is a core learning resource.

A **core learning resource** *is one that all students must experience in order to develop the understanding necessary to pass a course.*

A **supplementary learning resource** *is one that will help some students understand a course.*

Teachers should determine the extent to which resources developed specifically for a flexible learning environment can be used in other environments. In this way the maximum number of students and teachers will be helped, and therefore the return on investment will be maximized.

For example, potential uses of the strategic marketing package in environments other than the one it was specifically designed for include the following:

- Students studying the same course, but with compulsory weekly lecture and tutorial attendance. In this situation the teacher may distribute parts of the package that explain concepts that many students find difficult to understand.
- Students studying strategic marketing at a more advanced level. We all know that people do not remember everything they have studied, so why not place copies of the package in a library to remind students of course material from previous years?
- As a resource to help teachers prepare for lectures and tutorials.

These are a few of the ways in which the return on investment can be maximized. It may seem obvious to try to use resources in as many situations as possible. However, I believe that all too often, resources are restricted to specific student groups and teachers. Why does this happen? Some reasons are as follows.

Staff not directly involved in a flexible learning project can see it as something radically different from campus-based environments that involve lectures and tutorials. They argue that if the environment is different, then how can any resources—such as paper packages and Web sites—developed as part of a flexible learning project be of use to them and their students? Overcoming this belief involves developing a sense of project ownership among staff and giving all staff copies of the resources.

Teachers and managers often see physical learning resources—that is, resources you can hold in your hands—as jewels to be guarded and distributed only to a select audience. I disagree. Instead, the jewels are teachers. What they bring to the physical resources, how they integrate them, and how they keep them up-to-date and interact with students is the competitive advantage of an institution. Locking away resources is contrary to the idea of maximizing the return on investment.

---

*An **institution** is an educational establishment that employs teachers, also called lecturers and academics, to help students develop their understandings of content. The content is categorized and presented as courses, also called subjects. A number of courses form a program of study.*

The argument of high distribution costs can be used to justify the decision to limit the use of a learning resource to a specific student group. However, if a resource is to be used in a supplementary manner, teachers can identify and distribute selected parts. Also, providing each student with a copy is not always necessary. What is necessary is that students are made aware of the resource and where they can use it.

TOPIC 1.3: INTRODUCING THE CASE STUDY

Throughout this handbook, a case study is presented that shows the application of the strategies and guidelines described in the chapters. The case study is a flexible learning project that I was involved in for four years. It occurred at The Hong Kong Polytechnic University's School of Hotel and Tourism Management, and is referred to as the HTM Project. I was the project manager and educational designer.

Your understanding of the HTM Project will develop as you read the handbook. In this topic, the case study is introduced by describing the project's aim, objectives, and setting, and outlining the characteristics of the resources developed.

Project Title

The Hotel and Tourism Management Flexible Learning Project (HTM Project).

Project Aim

To develop a flexible learning environment for the program of study titled Bachelor of Arts (Honors) in Hotel and Catering Management (Part-Time).

The program was full-fee paying and, therefore, students paid a set amount for each course. That is, the school received no direct financing from the university.

Project Objectives

1. To provide students with a learning environment in which they decide when to attend on-campus classes
   1.1. The development of print-based core learning resources for ten courses
2. To maximize the return on investment in the HTM Project by developing Internet-based learning resources, derived from the core learning resources developed for use in the Bachelor of Arts (Honors) in Hotel and Catering Management (Part-Time) program, for use as supplementary resources in other programs of study

The Bachelor of Arts (Honors) in Hotel and Catering Management (Part-Time) Program of Study

Program Aims

The programme [aims to provide] the undergraduate final year programme of the "sister" full-time programme . . . to those holders of a Higher Diploma from the host department all of whom have post-course practical experience in the industry. The programme [aims to] inculcate the student with knowledge, skills and professional attitudes needed to create value-added service for customers and with the ability to take on challenging managerial responsibilities in Hong Kong's competitive hotel and catering industry. (HTM, 2000)

List of Courses

The HTM Project involved ten courses:

1. Introduction to Business Law
2. Introduction to Economics
3. Quantitative Methods for Business
4. Hospitality Information Technology and e-Business
5. Hotel and Catering Services Management
6. Hotel and Catering Strategic Human Resource Management
7. Strategic Marketing in Hospitality and Tourism
8. Financial Management in Hospitality and Tourism
9. Hotel and Catering Operations Management
10. Strategic Management in Hospitality and Tourism

Length of Study

The majority of students took two years (part-time) to complete the courses. Students studied three courses in each of the first two semesters. Two courses were completed in each of the second-year semesters. Each semester was seventeen weeks long. Fourteen of these weeks were defined as course content weeks; one week was allocated to revision and two weeks were set aside for examinations for all courses.

*The word **semester** is used to denote a period of time in which students start and complete the study of a course.*

Some institutions use alternative descriptions, such as "terms," "trimesters," and "study periods."

Characteristics of Students in the Bachelor of Arts (Honors) in Hotel and Catering Management (Part-Time) Program

Between thirty-five and forty students enrolled in the program of study during each academic year. Some characteristics of those who enrolled in the program follow:

- The students' ages were between twenty and forty-five, with the majority being between twenty and twenty-nine years old.
- A minimum of six months working experience in the hotel and catering industry or a related industry was required.
- The majority of students worked full-time in the hotel and catering industry or a related industry.
- The majority of students had completed a higher diploma in the Hotel and Tourism Management School at the university.

Project Timelines

Table 1.1 illustrates the development and use timelines for the print-based flexible learning packages developed in accordance with HTM Project Objective 1. The ten course Web sites created in accordance with HTM Project Objective 2 were developed during Year 4 of the project.

The Learning Resources Developed

The features of the learning resources developed for each of the ten courses are described throughout this handbook. The following is a short description of the resources.

The general features of each print-based learning resource that was developed for each course, in accordance with Objective 1.1, are as follows.

- Each resource had between 400 and 500 pages, packaged in a file.
- The materials were divided into a course outline and twelve units of course content.
- Each unit focused on helping students achieve a list of learning objectives and included a number of topics.
- In addition to descriptions of content, presented using text and pictures, each topic included self-exercises and examples showing applications of the concepts.

TABLE 1.1. The Development and Use Timeline for the HTM Project Print-Based Flexible Learning Packages.

Course	Year 1 Semester 2	Year 2 Semester 1	Year 2 Semester 2	Year 3 Semester 1	Year 3 Semester 2	Year 4 Semester 1	Year 4 Semester 2
Hotel and Catering Services Management	Develop	Use	Use		Use	Use	
Hotel and Catering Strategic Human Resource Management		Develop	Use		Use		Use
Strategic Management in Hospitality and Tourism		Develop	Use	Use			Use
Introduction to Business Law		Develop	Develop	Use			Use
Introduction to Economics		Develop	Develop	Use		Use	
Strategic Marketing in Hospitality and Tourism			Develop	Use		Use	
Hotel and Catering Operations Management				Develop	Use		Use
Financial Management in Hospitality and Tourism					Develop	Use	
Hospitality Information Technology and e-Business					Develop	Use	
Quantitative Methods for Business					Develop		Use

A Web-based learning resource, derived from the corresponding print package, was developed for each course. This was for use as a supplementary resource in other programs of study, in accordance with Objective 2. The general features of the Web sites were as follows.

- The majority of the content in each course Web site was the same as that used in the corresponding print-based learning resource.
- The structure of a Web site, in terms of units and topics, was similar to that in the corresponding print-based learning resource.

- The navigational structure was designed to help students answer three questions users of Web sites often ask: Where am I? Where can I go? Where have I been?
- Self-exercises were modified to make use of the capabilities of the Internet.

TOPIC 1.4: THE DEVELOPMENT MODEL

The HTM Project development model was a work in progress for four years. It was during the journey from project conception to finalization that the model was tested and refined. In Topic 1.4 the results of this journey are presented. Although the model will be of interest to all people involved in a flexible learning project, the perspective from which it was developed is that of a project manager and educational designer.

The model is described

- to establish the framework upon which the case study—the HTM Project—is built;
- to provide an orientation to the structure of the handbook chapters;
- to describe a development model that is consistent with an organized chaos approach to project management (Topic 2.4); and
- to allow potential users to decide the usefulness of applying the model to your specific projects.

Figure 1.1 illustrates the development model that evolved during the HTM Project. Although your understanding of the model will develop as you read the handbook, the terminology and relationships are explained here.

The most important part of a learning resource is the quality of the content. A resource can be a pleasure to read because well-established design principles have been applied. However, if the words are not quality content, the resource is ineffective. A computer simulation may be designed on the basis of usability principles and the latest interactive technologies, but if the simulation is based on information that is not quality content, the resource is ineffective. So what is quality content?

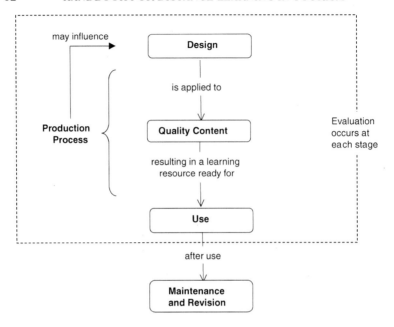

FIGURE 1.1. A Development Model for Flexible Learning Resources

Quality content *is information that is accurate and relates to the sections of the course syllabus for which the learning resource is being developed.*

Consider the two parts of the quality content definition—accuracy and relationship to the syllabus.

- Information is accurate if it is created by people recognized by the community as experts in their field of study. For example, university academics are usually experts in particular fields of study. And, a person who has been a front-office manager for many years is an expert in that field.
- Information that relates to the course syllabus is information that can be identified as relating to at least one of the course's learning objectives.

It cannot be taken for granted that the information in a learning resource is quality content. I believe that concentrating on design and production issues can result in insufficient effort being devoted to ensuring quality content. This is particularly the case with developments involving computers, in which a project team may focus on the latest technology to the detriment of the content.

The process of ensuring quality content is largely independent of the media used in the resource. Guidelines for ensuring quality content are presented in Topic 4.3.

Quality content is part of the development model. The other parts of the model are now defined.

---

*A **design**, described in a specification document, is applied to quality content. It has media-independent and media-dependent parts.*

***Production** is a process. It involves applying a design to quality content, resulting in the creation of a resource.*

The media-independent aspects of a design are discussed in Chapter 4. Chapters 5 to 9 discuss media-dependent issues.

***Use** occurs when the intended audience experiences a resource.*

***Evaluation** involves observing an environment to compare reality with intended outcomes.*

Evaluation occurs throughout the development model. That is, not only the use of a resource is evaluated. So too is the quality of the content, the design, and the production process. Formative evaluation approaches are emphasized in the development model so that continuous improvements are made.

***Maintenance** involves making small changes to any combination of the quality content, the design, and the production process.*

***Revision** involves changes to any combination of the quality content, the design, and the production process that are more significant than those associated with maintenance.*

Maintenance usually relates to matters affected by time. Examples of maintenance issues include semester dates, assignments that need changing for a new student group, and changing scenarios based upon local situations that no longer exist, such as a restaurant closing down that was the subject of an activity. Revision is usually an outcome of evaluating the use of a resource.

KEY POINTS

1. Flexible learning means different things to different people. Be aware of these differences and be able to write a definition that describes the environment you want to create.
2. When thinking about creating a flexible learning environment ask yourself the following questions: Who are you interested in providing choice for? What types of choices do you want to provide? How do you intend to provide them?
3. Resist the temptation to lock away flexible learning resources as if they are the jewels of your institution. They are not. Instead, maximize their usefulness by giving every teacher in your institution copies and asking them to think about how the resources may help them and their students.

Chapter 2

The Project Manager

Every project needs a manager. Depending on the project's complexity, this person may also have other roles within the team. A project manager needs to maintain the support of senior staff and be able to direct effective meetings.

Considering a project as organized chaos can help develop quality learning and teaching resources, as will the selective use of project management techniques and tools.

OBJECTIVES

1. To emphasize that regardless of the size of a project team, it is important that someone fulfills the roles of a project manager
2. To describe the roles and characteristics of a project manager, emphasizing the importance of good communication and people skills and the ability to maintain the support of senior staff
3. To provide guidelines for ensuring that meetings are effective
4. To provide advice for the novice project manager about the usefulness of project management aids, such as books and computer software programs
5. To describe how, by viewing a project as organized chaos, the project manager can maintain an emphasis on supporting the development of quality resources, rather than on control

TOPIC 2.1: EVERY PROJECT HAS A MANAGER

Although Chapter 2 is addressed to project managers, it will also be of interest to those responsible for appointing them. Projects come in all shapes and sizes, and they all need managers. A project can be

small enough that you are the only team member. For example, you may develop lecture notes or your own course Web site. At the other end of the scale are projects of such complexity that they need a team of people, one of whom is employed as the project manager. A university-wide implementation of a course management system is such a project.

The majority of project management books focus on large projects that employ a project manager. However, in educational settings, such as universities, teachers often complete projects by themselves and fulfill more than one role. For example, a teacher may act as a content writer, educational designer, and project manager, and work with a computer programmer on the development of a simulation exercise.

In this chapter I provide information useful to anyone starting a project, regardless of its complexity, with the goal of helping teachers teach and students learn.

A **project** is an activity with specific objectives and definite start and end dates.

A **project manager** plans and manages change. The person is responsible for ensuring a project is a success.

TOPIC 2.2: THE ROLES AND CHARACTERISTICS OF A PROJECT MANAGER

In this topic the roles and characteristics of a project manager are considered, the importance of senior staff support is emphasized, and strategies to encourage support are presented. The topic concludes by considering how to hold effective meetings.

Every project needs a manager. The more complex and innovative the project, the greater the need for the person to

- have experience in managing change in educational institutions;
- have project management qualifications; and
- be involved in the project only as the manager.

In reality most projects involve a manager who is either responsible for many projects or has multiple roles within a project. For example, in a project to develop four new courses, the project team may consist of four teachers, as content writers, and an educational designer who is also the project manager. Delegating one person for each position in a project team is not a prerequisite for success. What is a prerequisite is that someone fulfills the role of a project manager.

A project manager

- plans, by asking six questions about each part of a project (What? Why? When? Where? How? Who?);
- decides what resources are necessary, and manages them to make sure the budget is not exceeded;
- is a motivator, helping to keep the project team focused;
- helps meetings be effective by ensuring that they are focused, and that all people's views are heard, and decisions are made;
- keeps a project moving by making sure that things are done once a decision is made;
- delegates work to other team members and gives people the resources and support they need; and
- is a publicist, ensuring that people know about the project's progress and that they support it.

An effective project manager should be

- approachable, that is, someone people feel is open and accessible;
- logical and organized, yet with a high tolerance for uncertainty;

- someone who knows when to listen rather than talk;
- able to evaluate and make a decision from information gathered from many sources;
- trustworthy, that is, someone who people can trust and who, having given someone a task, is willing to trust that the job will be done; and
- able to multitask, that is, to think about and do many things during each day.

As stated previously, a project manager should be an approachable person, someone who people are comfortable meeting with, volunteering information to, and discussing personal matters with. However, there is a balancing act between being approachable and fulfilling the roles of a project manager. A manager has to make sure that decisions are made, publicized, and enacted. A manager is not there to be a nice person all the time. Decisions will have to be made that do not please all team members.

Maintaining the Support of Senior Staff

Project management is always challenging, but in an academic environment, such as a university, it can be *very* challenging. Academic freedom is an essential part of educational institutions. However, it can be used as an excuse for an inability to enact decisions and to produce materials on time. Without the visible support of the head of the school and other senior staff, the challenges a manager faces can be too great.

A **school,** also called a department, is part of an institution. The school staff specialize in a discipline of study such as hotel and tourism management.

It is therefore important to make sure senior staff know how a project is progressing. They cannot support something about which they know little. Some strategies for keeping senior staff informed of project progress include the following:

- Hold monthly meetings with senior staff.
- Before a monthly meeting, distribute a progress report to senior staff. This will encourage staff to prepare and provide a focus for the meeting.

- Make senior staff aware of any project publicity that appears outside the school, for example, in an institution's newsletter or a newspaper.
- All written communication to senior staff should be concise and designed for quick reading.

Once aware of project progress, senior staff must be seen to support it. For example, if culturally appropriate, senior staff can publicly congratulate team members on milestones reached and publicize the project within their leadership group (see Exhibit 2.1).

Holding Effective Meetings

A meeting is effective if people discuss issues, make decisions, and then enact the decisions. During the HTM Project I organized hundreds of meetings, ranging from those with only one other person to some involving more than twenty people. Because meetings play such a crucial role in projects, a number of strategies for ensuring their success should be remembered.

EXHIBIT 2.1. Head of School Support

The one person outside of the project team that was most crucial to the success of the HTM Project was the head of the school.

I was fortunate that the initiator of the project was head of the school. He also played a key role in my appointment as project manager and educational designer. Therefore, I started with a high level of support and ensured, through strategies such as those listed in the text, that this was maintained.

The head of the school often talked to staff at the start of my regular presentations about project progress, and appointed the project's content writers after consulting with myself and senior staff. Developing learning and teaching resources is a challenging and time-consuming activity. A meeting between the teacher, who was asked to be a content writer, and the head of the school helped in committing the teacher to the project.

It was through such actions that it became evident to staff that being involved in developing the resources was considered by senior management as a valued contribution to a staff member's teaching portfolio.

Before the Meeting

- *Is a meeting necessary?* Only organize a meeting when a number of issues or a complex issue need to be discussed. Too many meetings will slow a project down.
- *Distribute an advanced organizer.* Four days before a meeting, distribute an advanced organizer. In this short document list the objectives of the meeting, emphasizing any decisions to be made.
- *Meet away from offices.* If you are meeting with people who tend to be interrupted, hold the meeting away from their offices.
- *Discuss before the meeting.* If the meeting is being called to make a significant decision then informally discuss the issue with people beforehand.

- *Arriving late.* People arriving late cause problems. To encourage people to arrive on time you should arrive five minutes early and contact people as soon as they are late. For people with a history of arriving late, visit their offices as you go to the meeting.

During the Meeting

- *Focus.* Use the advanced organizer to focus the meeting.
- *Obtain views and discuss.* Ensure that all those who wish to speak do so. There will always be "refiners," "resonators," and "rebutters." Your people management skills can be tested; ensure that all views are heard. Resist the tendency to favor resonators—people who constantly agree with your opinions.
- *Once a decision is made, make sure everyone knows exactly what the decision is.* Be sure that when people leave a meeting, they cannot say they were unaware that a decision had been made.
- *Recognize when it is time to move on.* Keep the meeting moving by recognizing that sometimes an issue is too complex to be resolved in one meeting. Say that you will summarize the discussion in the meeting notes and that discussion will continue in the next meeting.
- *Finish on time.* If your meetings are known to be unfocused and go overtime, you will have increasing difficulty in getting people to attend. Therefore, never go into overtime and sometimes finish early.

After the Meeting

- *"Meeting finished" implies that it is time to write the minutes.* Write the minutes of the meeting as soon as possible and always within twenty-four hours. The longer this is left undone, the more is forgotten. Use the advanced organizer as the template for the minutes. Highlight any decisions, including any actions necessary, and by when and by whom the actions need to be completed.
- *Distribute minutes.* Distribute the minutes and make clear the date by which people have to respond with suggested modifications.

- *Finalize minutes.* Modify the minutes on the basis of feedback and distribute the final version.
- *Review your performance.* The more meetings you hold the better you will become at facilitation and knowing the personalities of participants. Review your performance by asking yourself, "What could I have done better?"

The more people are aware of the issues before a meeting, the better. You do not want people attending a meeting without knowing what is going to be discussed. Organizing an effective meeting is an art, rather than a science. It depends on your skills as project manager and the personalities of the participants. The strategies just presented are what I believe to be the essentials. That is, they are designed to avoid the all-too-common scenario of unfocused meetings that start late, finish late, are dominated by a few people, and the minutes of which are distributed one month later when people have forgotten what was discussed.

TOPIC 2.3: PROJECT MANAGEMENT AIDS

Many products are described as essential project management aids by those with an interest in selling the products. However, before buying anything it is worthwhile to reflect upon the context the project manager works in, the skills the manager needs, and which skills are already sufficiently developed.

As discussed previously, many flexible learning projects involve people working as the project manager on a part-time basis and without graduate-level project management expertise. For example, the content writer may also be the project manager. The educational designer may also fulfill this role. These people do not have the time, nor in most cases, the need, to develop expertise equivalent to a professional project manager. What these people need is a foundation-level understanding of project management and an awareness of the tools that can help. The first-time project manager should consider the usefulness of project-management aids. The following steps are helpful in reviewing such materials:

- *Find a good project management book.* Read an introductory project management book that discusses the fundamentals without direct reference to specific computer software products, and use the book as a reference throughout the project.
- *Consult a critical friend.* Find someone with project management experience who can act as your critical friend. This person critiques your work, considers the effect you are having on colleagues, and asks questions to encourage self-reflection and improvement (Costa and Kallick, 1993).
- *Experiment with computer software.* Experiment with project management software during the initial stages of a project so you can decide whether to continue or stop using the software. In this case your experiments will not be wasted, as often such experimentation helps you understand the principles discussed in project management books (Exhibit 2.2).
- *Maintain a diary.* Documentation of decisions and project progress is important. Therefore, maintain a diary as it will provide a written record and help your planning.
- *Do not hesitate to use pen and paper.* Remember, pen and paper have existed for centuries because they are convenient and useful. You do not have to use a computer to be an effective manager.

EXHIBIT 2.2. Using Project Management Software

Infatuation

Why did I try to use a popular project management computer program at the start of the HTM Project? First, I equated good management with using software. Second, I thought that in order to be seen as a project manager I had to use computer software. Third, I believed it would improve my productivity.

So, I studied the instructions, completed the tutorials, and developed a project timeline. The timeline was very colorful, contained lots of symbols for critical points and milestones, and looked very professional when printed out and placed in a prominent location in my office.

Reality

For three months I updated the timeline based on meeting notes and project progress. I found myself spending more and more time maintain-

(continued)

(continued)

ing the timeline and its associated tables. I used the software less as I felt that keeping both a handwritten project diary and the software up-to-date was an ineffective use of time. I stopped using the software. Instead my diary became my main project record and aid.

Lessons Learned

I do not regret using the project management software. It was useful being able to apply the techniques and understand the concepts discussed in the project management book I was reading. However, with time I accepted that pen and paper are a lot more convenient and portable than a computer.

TOPIC 2.4: THE PROJECT AS ORGANIZED CHAOS

A project manager can have too much control, such as wanting to know what each team member is doing every hour of every day. At the other extreme the manager can have a carefree approach where anything goes as long as the project ends on time. I recommend neither of these approaches. Instead, I see project management as organized chaos. Describing some of my experiences with the HTM Project will elucidate what I mean (see Exhibit 2.3).

Although I am arguing against a babysitter approach to project management, the manager and educational designer need to encourage writers to contact them if necessary. There needs to be an open-door approach that allows project members to decide when to visit.

Acceptance of some disorder, and letting go of the need to know everything about a project's progress, have advantages:

- A trusting environment is created where team members feel they are valued as professionals.
- Creative solutions to helping students learn are more likely to develop in environments where people have freedom to experiment and deadlines are not the only focus.
- As a project manager, being willing to concentrate on the big picture and not micromanage can be a lot healthier. Management is stressful enough without creating unnecessary worries.

EXHIBIT 2.3. There Is No Need to Know Everything

At the start of the development of a course package, the content writers and I agreed upon a timetable. This table listed dates by which I was to receive drafts and redrafts of the twelve units in a print-based package. On average, deadlines were set every two weeks.

I decided to ask a writer about progress only if I had not received a draft by the agreed date. My reasons were that I did not need to know every detail about how each unit was going. For example, I did not need to know that with only four days to go until a deadline, a writer had yet to start. What mattered was that we developed quality materials. Such an approach also meant that I could meet informally with writers, for example at lunch, without them worrying that I was going to remind them of approaching deadlines.

An organized chaos approach to management recognizes that each writer is an individual, with different professional and personal responsibilities. For example, one writer would always submit first drafts about a week behind schedule. The first time this occurred we had a short meeting so I could express my concern and check if there were any problems. There were none. The writer said I would have the draft within five days. The draft was of such good quality that my input as an educational designer was minimal and only small amounts of redrafting were necessary. From this point onward I knew that this writer could be given some timetable flexibility. I do not know how the writer wrote such quality material so quickly. The fact is, I did not need to know. Instead I admired the writer's skills and accepted a different way of achieving our objective of producing quality resources in time for the start of the semester.

The following are some guidelines for implementing an organized chaos approach:

- *Some ignorance is good.* Accept that you do not need to know everything about the project. What matters is that the resources developed are of high quality and are produced in time for students to use.
- *Think like a shark—keep moving!* Sharks die if they stop moving, as they need water to be flowing across their gills. Projects are similar. At the end of every week you need to be able to see some progress. Once a project stops it is hard to get it moving again.
- *Be flexible.* A missed deadline is usually not the end of the world. The only ultimate deadline is the date that students start

the course. So when a deadline is missed find out why, see if the people involved need help, and set a new deadline.

- *Stay calm.* A project manager who publicly expresses anger will find it harder to maintain a creative and effective team environment.
- *Keep weeks in reserve.* Before meeting with people to set deadlines, ask yourself what is the latest date by which the resource needs to be 100 percent complete. Do not tell anyone this date. Instead, set a public "final" date that is three weeks earlier. Doing this allows you to have reserve weeks in case of unexpected events.
- *Remember that everyone is unique.* Each team member should try to accept that his or her colleagues are unique. Every person has a different perspective and personal responsibilities, and achieves objectives in different ways.

KEY POINTS

1. You may have a project on which you are the only person involved. In such a situation, you are your own project manager.
2. A project manager should be an approachable person who respects variety among people and is able to make decisions.
3. The ultimate objective of a project is to produce quality learning resources by the time students need them. The path toward this objective does not have to be straight and tightly controlled.

Chapter 3

Starting a Project

A flexible learning project results from recognizing that a learning and teaching environment can be improved or that a potential new market exists. A mix of purchased and developed resources can be used. Once a decision is made to develop resources, the project team is formed and stakeholder meetings are held to establish the project's scope. Encourage a sense of project ownership beyond the stakeholders. To ensure that content writers have a strong commitment to a project, they need to be aware of the advantages and challenges of developing flexible learning resources.

OBJECTIVES

1. To describe how the decision to start a project is the result of someone deciding a need exists to develop a flexible learning environment to either improve a situation or develop a new market
2. To list and discuss factors to consider when deciding the extent to which resources are developed and the extent to which they are purchased
3. To describe the roles and skills of project team members, emphasizing that often a person fills more than one role
4. To explain the role of stakeholder meetings in establishing the scope of a project and to list issues to be discussed in such meetings and strategies to ensure they are successful
5. To emphasize the importance of encouraging a sense of project ownership and to list techniques to encourage it
6. To list questions that teachers should use to self-appraise their ability and willingness to be involved in a project
7. To describe potential rewards for teachers of being involved as content writers in flexible learning projects

TOPIC 3.1: THE SPARK

A project is an attempt to satisfy an unmet need or want. In relation to a teaching and learning environment, it reflects either a desire to improve a situation or a potential new market.

Not all projects that occur in educational institutions are aimed directly at helping students. For example, an academic may start a research project with the goal of ultimately publishing a journal article, thereby enhancing his or her research portfolio, or he or she may decide to develop a teaching portfolio to include with employment applications. Both these examples can have the indirect benefit of helping students learn. In the first example, the academic may discuss the research findings in courses. In the second example, developing teaching portfolios encourages academics to critique their skills and identify areas that need professional development.

In this handbook the focus is on projects where the main goal is to help students. In particular, it focuses on projects that develop a flexible learning environment where there is a range of learning resources and students have some control over which resources they use, when they use them, and how they use them.

A project can involve only one person and does not have to be large. For example, you may be a teacher, and the spark for your one-person project is your belief that adding summaries of Web sites to tutorial notes will encourage students to use the Internet. Alternatively, the project can be large and complex, such as a university-wide implementation of a course management system. Here the spark can be the belief, at the senior management level, that such a system can help students and increase the competitive advantage of the university. Another large project is the HTM Project, presented as the case study in this handbook (Exhibit 3.1).

TOPIC 3.2: DEVELOPING AND BUYING RESOURCES

Place yourself in the following situation. You believe that a need exists to improve the learning and teaching environment. This can involve increasing the range of learning resources. The question is: To what extent do you develop resources and to what extent do you buy resources?

When answering this question, you need to consider the characteristics of the students, the teachers, and the overall teaching and learn-

EXHIBIT 3.1. The Spark

As described in Topic 1.3, the goal of the HTM Project was to develop a flexible learning environment for a number of courses studied by part-time students working in the hotel and tourism industry.

The program of study had previously required students to obtain employer permission to attend one full day of classes each week. Obtaining this permission was difficult and not always possible. The hours of work vary in the hotel and tourism industry and often staff are needed on short notice. In addition, in an environment of increasing economic uncertainty, students were understandably reluctant to request special treatment.

Therefore, a need existed to develop a teaching and learning environment that better integrated with students' jobs. This resulted in the main objective of the HTM Project—to develop an environment in which students decided when to attend on-campus classes. The school wanted to support choice in attendance.

ing environment. Various factors must be considered when deciding between developing or buying.

Prepurchase Considerations

- *Consider the extent to which the content of the resource matches the syllabus.* Some variation between the content of the resource and the course syllabus can be good. What is important is that before listing it as a core resource, and therefore recommending students buy it, the teacher is confident that the majority of students will make extensive use of it. Otherwise, make it a supplementary resource and explore ways of making it available for students on loan.
- *Integration with the existing teaching and learning environment is important.* Think about how you can integrate the resource with the existing environment. For example, to what extent can you encourage students to use the resource by recommending parts of it throughout the lecture notes you distribute?
- *Does the resource help you offer a variety of perspectives using a variety of media?* Consider the extent to which the resource adds variety to the perspectives offered and the media used by students. From a constructivist perspective, such variety is important.
- *How many of the examples will be familiar to students?* Think about the extent to which the examples used in the resource are applicable to the students' lives. For example, a resource about opening a restaurant that includes a large section on the size of parking lots relative to customer turnover has little relationship to the situation in Hong Kong.

Predevelopment Considerations

- *Development takes time and your resources.* Before committing to developing a resource, consider the financial and nonfinancial costs to yourself.
- *Think about what only you can offer students.* Have an understanding of the resources you can buy. This will help you think about how best you can offer unique information in a resource you develop. Remember, your thoughts, experiences, and interpretations are valuable to students.

- *Promote integration and variety.* Consider how your resource would integrate with the existing teaching and learning environment and how it would add variety to the perspectives offered and the media used.
- *Can you target student difficulties?* You should offer students experiences that purchased resources do not offer, that is, learning opportunities based on your understanding of the capabilities of the students, their needs, and their wants. Why develop a resource that offers students the same opportunities they can get from purchased resources?

I recommend an approach that offers students a range of learning resources obtained from a variety of sources. For example, a course may have notes written by the teacher, a textbook, and may involve students referring to recommended Web sites, the local library, and newspapers. Such a range of learning resources, offering a variety of perspectives, helps students learn. This is consistent with a constructivist approach to education, as discussed in Topic 4.2.

One type of learning resource should be part of all courses—notes written by the teacher. I mentioned in Topic 1.2 that the jewels of an educational institution, that is, its competitive advantage, are the teachers. As part of making their thoughts, experiences, and interpretations available to students, notes written by the teachers should be distributed. The purpose, extent, and medium used, for example, paper-based or Web-based, for these notes will vary depending on factors such as what other resources are available, and the money and time available. Students should "hear" the voices of their teachers (see Exhibit 3.2).

TOPIC 3.3: THE PROJECT TEAM

The goal of this topic is to help you decide who should be members of a project team. A project team often consists of one person. For example, many teachers are one-person teams when they develop a Web site to support their course lectures and tutorials. Alternatively, a project involving many courses can involve many people, some of whom move in and out of the team as needed.

EXHIBIT 3.2. Why Learning Resources Were Developed

The HTM Project involved developing and buying resources. Three of the ten courses included a purchased textbook as a core resource. Every course had a developed, paper-based package as a core resource. Through the packages, students could "hear" their teachers' voices and read materials that included examples relevant to their lives.

The aim of the HTM Project, and its objectives, as well as the lack of existing core learning resources meant that the materials developed needed to be comprehensive. The budget and time available meant that high-quality teacher-written notes could be developed. The result was a paper-based package of between 400 and 500 pages for each course.

One of my design objectives was to ensure that each course contextualized the content so that students could see the concepts and techniques being applied in their professional and social environments. For example, local restaurants were often mentioned. As were small and large Hong Kong–based hotel and tourism companies. Students need to be able to answer the question: How does this relate to my world?

It was important to contextualize in this way as the majority of textbooks, Web sites, and videos that could be used as core or supplementary resources were based on overseas contexts. This is not to say that overseas examples are not important. However, I believe that too many of the resources Hong Kong students use come from overseas, and, consequently, lack contextualization. Developing packages was an opportunity to address this imbalance.

A ***project team*** *consists of people fulfilling the positions necessary for project success. Each position has roles, and in order to fulfill the roles a person needs certain skills.*

I recommend a two-step approach to team formation. First, decide the positions that need to be filled. Second, while recognizing that a person may have more than one position, find people with the skills necessary to fill the positions.

Three positions that I consider to be essential in any flexible learning project are

1. content writer,
2. project manager, and
3. educational designer.

Some positions are necessary in certain projects depending on the objectives including:

• editor,
• development officer,
• peer reviewer,
• graphic designer,
• Web designer,
• computer programmer,
• webmaster, and
• project assistant.

Project management and educational design experts often promote a large-team approach as a criterion for project success. I disagree. What is most important is that the positions necessary for project success are filled (see Exhibit 3.3). One person may fill more than one position because he or she wants to and has the necessary skills or because money is limited. The issues of desire and money play a significant part in the formation of project teams.

• *Desire:* Not everyone wants to involve other people in a project. For example, a teacher may wish to fill all, or many, of the positions associated with developing a course Web site. Whether this approach works depends on factors such as the project's objectives and the teacher's ability to learn required skills. Such teachers should be encouraged rather than told they must use a team approach. Moreover, they need to be aware of what specialist help is available.

- *Money:* A major project cost is the wages of team members. Teachers designing course Web sites may prefer to employ specialists, such as Web designers. However, the money to do so is not always available.

By placing too much emphasis on a team approach, we run the risk of discouraging motivated people from experimenting and creating.

When forming a project team, the following points should be kept in mind:

- The project manager, in consultation with senior management, should determine who is on the team.
- Team members can change because people join as required and leave once their roles are completed.
- A person can successfully fill more than one position.
- A large project may need more than one person to fill some positions. For example, a project to develop Web sites for thirty courses may involve three educational designers.

EXHIBIT 3.3. The Project Team

Two team members were involved in the development of all print-based packages and Web sites for the ten courses in the HTM Project. For the print-based packages, I acted as the project manager, educational designer, editor, staff development officer, and graphic designer; and another person acted as a project assistant, educational designer, staff development officer, and graphic designer. In addition, during the development of the ten Web sites, which occurred after all print-based packages were developed, we also acted as Web designers.

Each course involved at least one peer reviewer, and for the first five print-based packages developed, an additional project assistant was employed. The number of content writers depended on factors such as the extent to which one academic had expertise across an entire syllabus and the workloads of school academics. Five courses each had one content writer, three each had two writers, one course had six writers, and one had seven. For seven of the ten courses, content writers were involved for which the language of instruction, English, was their second language.

In Topic 2.2 the roles and skills of a project manager are considered. Other project positions will be described, with an emphasis on the content writer and educational designer, which are essential in a flexible learning project.

Roles and Skills of a Content Writer

A **content writer** *is the principal author of the material used to create a learning resource. The person is responsible for ensuring quality content, that is, information that is accurate and relevant to the course syllabus.*

A content writer

- ensures that a course syllabus is relevant to the program of study;
- writes course notes that are conceptually accurate;
- makes sure that all course notes relate to the syllabus, and that these relationships are explicit enough to allow students to use learning objectives to guide their study; and
- acts as a quality controller to ensure that all activities, computer simulations and animations, for example, developed in conjunction with other project team members are conceptually accurate and are designed on the basis of an understanding of the common conceptual difficulties that students have.

A person needs certain characteristics to be able to fill the role of a content writer. Such a person should be

- recognized by peers as having an expert understanding of the conceptual foundations of the course;
- familiar with the course syllabus, and preferably experienced at teaching the course to students with backgrounds similar to those of the flexible learning students;
- willing and able to commit to months of writing, which involves continued development of one's understanding of course concepts and educational design guidelines;
- able to accept the critiques of educational designers and fellow content experts who are acting as peer reviewers; and

- able to communicate with people who are not course-content experts about how to modify learning activities to better meet the needs and wants of students.

Roles and Skills of an Educational Designer

*An **educational designer** applies learning and teaching design principles to the development of learning resources. The person is responsible for ensuring that resources are based upon an understanding of general educational foundations, the needs and wants of flexible learning students, and the capabilities of the media used.*

An educational designer

- works with a content writer and other members of the project team to create learning resources that include activities designed to help students develop their understandings of course concepts, including opportunities to self-test their understandings;
- ensures that resources include features designed to help students plan their study schedules and remain on track during the course;
- critiques the work of the content writer from an educational perspective;
- coordinates the peer-review process, which involves the consideration of a content writer's work by other content experts; and
- acts as a "student" by asking the following questions while reviewing developing resources: Why am I using this resource? Where am I? Where can I go? What have I seen? How does this relate to my world? How can I determine if I understand? What do other people think?

Certain characteristics are required to fill the role of an educational designer. Such a person should

- have an understanding of general educational design principles;
- have an understanding of the advantages and disadvantages of using particular media;

- be willing to quickly develop a foundation understanding of a course syllabus, including the terminology, so as to be better able to discuss matters with content writers;
- be inquisitive and interested in the world;
- have good communication skills and the ability to offer constructive criticism and work with people to improve resources; and
- be approachable, trustworthy, and diplomatic.

Roles and Skills of Other Project Positions

Some positions are necessary in certain projects. For example, an editor is important when the language used in the learning resource is not the primary language of the content writers. Often someone also acting as a project manager, content writer, or educational designer fills these positions (see Table 3.1).

As emphasized earlier, it is not a case of one person for every project position. Although it would be ideal to employ a specialist for each role, the reality is that people multitask. For example, a teacher developing a Web site may act as the content writer, project manager, and educational designer, and, by using computer software, act as the graphic designer, Web designer, and webmaster. In most educational institutions, members of a flexible learning project multitask.

TOPIC 3.4: STAKEHOLDER MEETINGS

A **stakeholder** can be any combination of the following:

- *A person whose support is important to the success of the project*
- *A member of the project team*
- *A person whose responsibilities will change as a result of the project*

Although stakeholder meetings are usually held only for large projects, many of the issues discussed also need to be considered in smaller projects. The difference is that it occurs in a more informal and smaller setting. For example, if you are running a one-person project to develop a course Web site, you still need to think about the effect the project will have on your time, what development resources you need, and which students will have access to the site. Therefore,

TABLE 3.1. Positions Other Than Project Manager, Content Writer, and Educational Designer That Can Be Part of a Flexible Learning Project Team

Position	Description
Editor	Modifies drafts of course notes, concentrating on grammatical issues
	An important position when the course language is not the primary language of the content writer
Development officer	Also known as a staff development officer or a professional development officer
	Responsible for the training and support of teachers working in a flexible learning environment
	In many institutions, employed by a centralized teaching and learning department, which conducts professional development seminars for teachers
Peer reviewer	A person with an expert's understanding of the conceptual foundations of the course for which resources are being developed
	Critiques the course notes of a content writer, and through the educational designer, offers suggested changes
	Ideally, at least one reviewer should work in the same school as the content writer, allowing the content writer to meet with the reviewer to have informal discussions
Graphic designer	Responsible for the "look and feel" of the resource being developed
	The skills required depend on the resource's medium. Although certain fundamental principles are applicable to all media, medium-specific principles are also applicable. For example, design guidelines for print-based resources vary from those for Web sites.
Web designer	Responsible for the production of Web sites
	Increasingly being seen as also filling the position of graphic designer
Computer programmer	Responsible for the coding of activities that require specialist programming knowledge beyond that traditionally expected of Web designers
	Computer-based activities, such as simulations, that are not Web based and require coding in specialist computer languages
Webmaster	Responsible for the maintenance and revision of Web sites
Project assistant	Responsible for modifying electronic documents on the basis of changes made by content writers and educational designers
	Often the most multiskilled person on a project team
	Commonly fills many of the roles associated with other positions

although this topic focuses on stakeholder meetings for projects involving more than one course and more than one person, it has relevance to smaller projects.

The goal of stakeholder meetings is to establish the scope of a project. At the end of the meetings, the project manager must be confident that the project can proceed according to an agreed list of parameters, including a course development timetable that contains major milestones. For a project involving the development of a teaching and learning environment, I recommend that the following people attend the meetings:

- A meeting facilitator
- Senior management, such as the head of the school and assistant heads
- The leader and assistant leader of the program of study
- The chair of the school's teaching and learning committee
- The leader of the school's administration team responsible for the course program
- The following project team members: project manager, content writers, educational designers, and, if part of the team, project assistants, editors, development officers, peer reviewers, graphic designers, Web designers, computer programmers, and webmasters

It can be a challenge to achieve the right balance between not enough and too many people attending a meeting. Stakeholder meetings should involve no more than twenty people. It may appear that the list of recommended people contains more. However, you will find that attendees often have multiple roles. For example, the chair of the teaching and learning committee may also be a content writer. Also, not all project team members may be identified at this early project stage.

Members of the project team should attend, including people such as editors, graphic designers, Web designers, and computer programmers. Such people can benefit from hearing the concerns and issues of educationalists, such as content writers and educational designers. Educationalists benefit equally from developing an understanding of the perspectives of people such as editors and programmers. Too many artificial barriers exist between professions. Breaking these barriers helps maximize the sense of project ownership.

The decision to include students who are currently completing the program of study in the stakeholder meetings is debatable. There is no doubt that their views should be sought, however, I believe that stakeholder meetings are not the appropriate place to express them. Some of the issues discussed are confidential, and participants may be reluctant to raise their concerns in the presence of students. The issue of students attending meetings is related to the cultural expectations of students and teachers. In your environment, it may well be best if student representatives attend.

A facilitator runs the stakeholder meetings. It is best if the facilitator is not a project stakeholder and is employed outside of the school. This gives objectivity to the meeting dynamics as the facilitator is independent of the project and concentrates solely on organizing and running the meeting. To ensure that the meeting is focused, the facilitator needs to work closely with the project manager. Depending on the facilitator's familiarity with flexible learning and the history of the school, it may be necessary for the facilitator and the project manager to act as cohosts.

Issues discussed in stakeholder meetings include the following:

- *What type of flexibility?* The types of flexibility that are possible and the types that stakeholders want to provide need to be discussed.
- *The curriculum structure.* The curriculum structure of the program of study needs to be considered. This includes discussing the extent to which the teaching and learning environment will differ from existing environments and the consequences. For example, changes may need to be approved by the institution's senior management and courses may have to be revalidated. Issues to be discussed include (1) the syllabi, whether differences from existing courses are allowed and desired; (2) the student attendance model; and (3) the assessment structure.
- *The development timetable.* A timetable of project development should be an outcome of stakeholder meetings. This timetable includes major milestones, such as the dates by which course resources must be ready for use.

- *Recognition of content writers.* Content writers are usually different from other project team members in that they are not involved only in projects. Often they are academics who also have teaching and research duties. A common concern of writers is how they will be rewarded for their efforts.
- *The impact of change.* Consider how changes in the teaching and learning environment will affect students, teachers, and administrative staff. To what extent will additional financial and nonfinancial resources be necessary?
- *Facilitators and inhibitors.* Facilitators and inhibitors of project success should be discussed. For inhibitors, it is important to consider ways in which their effects can be minimized.
- *Remember the students currently enrolled.* The impact of the changes on currently enrolled students has to be considered. For example, is it ethical to change the environment for currently enrolled students?

The following are strategies for managing stakeholder meetings:

- *Number of meetings.* Hold two or three meetings rather than one all-day meeting, and allow about two weeks between meetings. This will allow the minutes to be distributed and the project manager and facilitator to plan.
- *Success is often determined by what occurs before meetings.* The project manager and facilitator need to work closely together. Meetings must be planned and summarized. The project manager must discuss issues with stakeholders before a meeting.
- *Encourage participation.* The facilitator must encourage all stakeholders to participate. Having small-group activities is one way of encouraging participation. Another is for the facilitator to direct questions to participants who have yet to speak. Everyone must leave the meeting feeling that his or her contribution has been valued.
- *Have a variety of activity types.* For example, encourage role-playing, small-group activities, and general discussions. In particular, dividing people into small groups and assigning one person from each group to present results is recommended. Ensure that each group has a mix of people. For example, ideally, you

do not want all content writers, or all Web designers, in one group.

- *Evaluate a meeting and improve.* Distribute a feedback questionnaire with the minutes of a meeting. The responses provide valuable feedback and identify issues that people feel are not resolved. Do not ask people to complete a questionnaire just before leaving a meeting. At such times people are eager to leave and their responses will be rushed.

The following case study discussion of the HTM Project stakeholder meetings is presented in three parts:

1. A general discussion of the meetings
2. The major outcomes of the meetings, that is, establishing the scope of the HTM Project
3. A discussion of the types of flexibility the HTM Project was designed to facilitate

The Stakeholder Meetings

Two three-hour stakeholder meetings were held three weeks apart. Fifteen people, including a facilitator, attended. My roles were cofacilitator, project manager, and educational designer.

At the start of the first meeting the head of the school stated that the goal of the project was to develop a flexible learning environment where students decided when to attend on-campus classes. The aim of the meetings was to discuss how to achieve this. Topic 1.3 includes details about the project's objectives, the program of study, and the students.

Each participant was given a copy of the program-of-study document that described matters such as the existing curriculum and university regulations. This helped provide a focus as people could easily compare the existing situation with the changes that were to be made to create a flexible environment.

I found that activities involving groups of five people were useful in encouraging participation and ideas. One person from each group would present the group's findings to all participants.

As project manager, I worked with the facilitator before each meeting. The facilitator's knowledge about flexible learning helped to ensure that the meetings were a success. I recommend that when looking for a facilitator, you approach people who are working on similar projects in different institutions. This encourages a degree of impartiality while ensuring a knowledgeable person fills the role.

Between the meetings my role could be likened to that of a diplomat, discussing ideas and proposals with participants based upon the views expressed in the first meeting and in the feedback questionnaire. This helped in setting a focused agenda for the second meeting, when the scope of the project was finalized.

The Project Scope

This discussion of the scope of the HTM Project will be of interest to those wanting to know more about the foundations of this case study.

The Curriculum Structure

Equivalency with the existing part-time program of study had to be maintained for two reasons. First, it was important for the part-time students that the degree had the same standing as the degree completed by full-time students. Second, any significant changes to the syllabi would have required the program of study, that is, the ten courses, to be revalidated. This would have unacceptably delayed the project.

Two on-campus attendance schemes were designed: one for students yet to enroll and one for students who would be in the second of two years of study when the first flexible learning packs were ready. The schemes were as follows:

- For students entering the second year of study, every week included a standard three-hour lecture and tutorial sessions. Of these fourteen weeks, five weeks (1, 4, 8, 12, and 13) were compulsory attendance. In addition, every week had an optional two-hour consultation session.
- For students yet to start the two-year program of study, week 1 was compulsory on-campus three-hour attendance, weeks 4, 8, 12, and 13 strongly encouraged three-hour attendance, and all other weeks were optional two-hour-attendance consultation sessions.

The assessment structure of 60 percent assignments and 40 percent final exam was maintained.

The Development Timetable

It was agreed to convert each of the ten courses gradually to a flexible approach. This would allow the project team to learn from experience. Also, the existing commitments of the content writers made simultaneous development of all courses impossible. A draft development timetable was designed.

Recognition of the Needs of Currently Enrolled Students

Some students had completed the first of two years of study before any flexible learning resources were ready. It was considered unethical to radically alter their environment after they had enrolled. Therefore, if these students wanted to, they could attend the standard weekly on-campus lectures and tutorials, in addition to receiving the packages.

Recognition of Content Writers

In the stakeholder meetings there was discussion about how to recognize the contribution of content writers. It was useful for the head of the school to hear the concerns of teachers. Issues discussed included

- whether being a content writer was classified as a research activity, a teaching activity, or some combination of the two;
- whether release from other duties—for example, administration—would be a reward;
- whether content writers would be paid to complete the packages outside of work hours; and
- how being a content writer would be recognized by faculty and university management.

The Types of Flexibility the HTM Project Was Designed to Facilitate

Discussion in the HTM Project's stakeholder meetings about the types of student choice to support were based on the premise that the main objective was to provide a learning environment in which students decided when to attend on-campus classes (see Table 3.2).

TOPIC 3.5: MAXIMIZING PROJECT OWNERSHIP

At a minimum, project ownership is an awareness of the project's objectives and progress. At its maximum, ownership is a deep sense of commitment to ensuring the project is successful, based upon the realization that you have an important role in ensuring its success.

Although it is obvious that the project team and other stakeholders should have a strong sense of ownership, it may be less obvious to groups such as international institutions. Efforts should be made to maximize project ownership so that more people have an awareness of a project, thus the greater the benefits to the project team. Potential benefits of maximizing project ownership include the following:

- The project team will receive solicited and unsolicited advice, some of which will be of use.
- A project involves change. Some people in a school may feel threatened and react by attempting to ignore or undermine the

project. The more their colleagues have a sense of ownership, the greater the probability that such people will see the project as an opportunity, not a threat.

- The school will be seen as taking a proactive approach to teaching and learning issues.
- Funding sources, such as institutional teaching committees and government agencies, are more likely to support projects they understand.

The project team, and other stakeholders, have a responsibility to promote the project. A combination of the following techniques can encourage project ownership:

- Sending a monthly e-mail to school staff summarizing progress and asking for suggestions about issues that the project team is debating.
- Asking for ideas when presenting seminars. People appreciate their views being sought.
- Ensuring that school staff who are members of institutional committees are updated regularly about the project's progress.
- Developing a relationship with the institution's teaching and learning department. Often such departments contain specialists who can act as peer reviewers for the project and suggest improvements and alternative ways of achieving objectives.
- Maintaining a Web site where the project's goals, objectives, progress, and products are presented.
- Encouraging team members to join and contribute to Internet discussion forums. In addition, having the address of the project's Web site at the end of each team member's e-mail signature can promote interest (Exhibit 3.4).

TOPIC 3.6: CONSIDERATIONS BEFORE COMMITTING TO A PROJECT—A SELF-APPRAISAL FOR TEACHERS

Place yourself in the following situation. You are a teacher and have been asked to join a project team as a content writer. The objective is to develop flexible learning resources for a course that you

TABLE 3.2. Stakeholder Decisions Regarding Program Flexibility

Type of Student Choice	Decisions Made in Stakeholder Meetings
Attendance on campus	Week 1 is the only compulsory attendance week.
	Attendance is strongly encouraged in four of the fourteen weeks, with the preferred model being weeks 4, 8, 12, and 13.
	In other weeks, students are given the option to attend consultation sessions.
	The end-of-course examination will be held on campus.
Pace of learning	An implied pace will be evident through a suggested study schedule and the rate at which the teacher discusses the syllabus in on-campus classes.
	Each student chooses whether to study at the recommended pace.
Means of communication with the teacher	Each student selects a combination of the following means of communication: attending on-campus classes, phone, e-mail, or visiting the teacher's office.
Frequency of teacher contact	Students decide when to initiate contact with the teacher.
	The teacher will initiate contact when there are concerns about the progress of a student, such as the failure to submit an assignment.
Course content available	Core content will be provided in a print-based package; some courses also to include a textbook.
	Variability in the content is mainly restricted to assignments where students have a choice of case studies to consider.
Whether to study the course content	Each learning package to contain twelve units of material; at the start of each unit will be a list of learning objectives designed to help students decide the extent to which they already understand the material.
	Each topic in a unit to contain a self-exercise so that students can attempt to self-evaluate their understandings and therefore determine whether to study or restudy the topic.
Content sequence	An implied sequence will be evident through the sequence of units in the package, a suggested study schedule, and the sequence in which the teacher discusses the content during on-campus classes.
Assessment	The assessment weighting will be 60 percent assignments and 40 percent final examination.
	The teacher is to determine the number of assignments, ranging from two to four.

EXHIBIT 3.4. Encouraging Project Ownership

The HTM Project took four years. Efforts at promoting a sense of ownership beyond the stakeholders occurred mainly during the first year. This was when I needed to gain the maximum support for the project and address fears in the school and the university that the project's aim was to replace teachers with distance education resources.

The techniques I found most effective, and quick to implement, included sending monthly progress e-mails to school staff and presenting a seminar twice a year to the school, to which interested parties—such as the institution's teaching and learning department—were also invited. Through regular e-mails and meetings with senior school staff, I was able to keep people on institutional committees informed.

My attempts to maintain a project Web site and regularly contribute to Internet-based discussion forums were less successful. Although a Web site was established I did not have the time to maintain it. Therefore, like so many Web sites, it was created, publicized, and then neglected. So that this does not occur with your project, I recommend you give specific responsibility to a team member to maintain the Web site.

In retrospect, my attempts at maximizing project ownership went no further than the institutional community. My approach was to concentrate on the school in order to ensure staff were aware of the project. Therefore they could start to think about using the resources in courses they taught, thereby maximizing the return on investment.

have taught previously in an on-campus mode. What are the issues you need to think about before agreeing to join the team?

The majority of this topic is written for the academic and teacher for whom being a flexible learning content writer would be an extra responsibility, in addition to normal teaching and research roles (Exhibit 3.5).

When asking yourself questions about a project, remember that less than desirable answers to some questions does not mean you should not commit to a project. Instead, by asking the following questions you can identify potential difficulties and work to minimize them:

- *To what extent can you work with the project team members, and how experienced are they?* An indicator of the likelihood of project success is that team members can work together. Consider the work experiences of the project manager and the educational designer. These are people you, as a content writer, will work with frequently. Ask your colleagues for their opinions.

- *What if you are a one-person project team? Can you get help?* You may develop a resource by yourself. Before you start, identify people who can help you if you reach a stage where you need some expert advice. For example, talk to educational designers to let them know about your project and that you may need their help.

- *Can you devote the time?* You need to talk with the project manager about the time you will need to allocate and when you will be required. Compare the manager's recommendations to the estimates of your colleagues who have completed similar projects.

- *Do you have the required development resources?* As a content writer you are primarily responsible for developing quality content. In general, this involves technology no more complex than pen and paper and a word-processing computer program. However, you also have a responsibility to ensure that activities accurately portray course concepts and target student difficulties. Therefore, you need to be able to evaluate the activities that are developed, for example, videos, simulations, and animations. A situation where you need to go to someone else's computer is not good enough. You should be able to experience the resource in your own time and using your own technology.

- *To what extent do you have a personal commitment to flexible learning?* Think about the depth of your commitment to flexible learning. It may be new to you. Therefore, seek out colleagues who have taught in such environments. Another excellent source of information is educational journals within your professional field. You need to reflect on how teaching in a flexible learning environment will impact your role as a teacher. For example, how will it change the hours you devote and the quality of the interactions you have with students?

- *Are you prepared for critical appraisal of your efforts?* Developing resources can be uncomfortable as an educational designer and your peers, acting as reviewers, critique your work. Your colleagues may suggest content that should be added or improved. You need to be able to receive their advice and consider its merits. You need to accept that an educational designer will say such things as, "I don't understand this section"; "This part is confusing"; "You seem to contradict yourself"; "Can we design a different activity that better explains that concept?"

- *Are you prepared to see your work on people's bookshelves and computers?* Flexible learning resources are in the public domain more than lecture and tutorial notes. Great pleasure can be obtained from knowing that your work appears on other people's bookshelves and computers. However, this can also be a source of apprehension as the resources represent your professional standards.

- *Do you have sufficient understanding of the course content?* You may be surprised that teachers need to ask themselves this question. Surely if you are a course teacher you have the necessary understanding. Unfortunately this is not always the case. In my experience, once staff hear that a content writer is needed, people tend to suggest anyone but themselves. Although the project manager can encourage senior staff to be writers, the ultimate choice depends on factors such as the wishes of the head of the school, staff workloads, and the recommendations of senior staff. This tends to result in junior staff being assigned. In such a situation the teacher's content understanding may well be excellent. However, junior staff members usually have a less well-developed understanding. In such cases, teachers need to appraise their level of understanding, consider the extent to which they need to develop it, and recommend that their colleagues with more experience are assigned as peer reviewers.

- *Who will have copyright on the resources?* Many resources are developed for which copyright issues are unresolved. This is a topic that content writers have an interest in.

- *What are the potential rewards?* Developing resources can be rewarding professionally and personally. Think about the rewards that you want.

Rewards

Usually a content writer is also fulfilling other duties. For example, an academic in a university may be a teacher, a researcher, and an administrator. This is in contrast to other project team members, who, in many cases, are employed to fulfill one role. For example, a computer

EXHIBIT 3.5. Convincing Teachers to Be Content Writers

Although the head of the school appointed academics to be content writers, as the HTM Project manager and an educational designer, I was responsible for ensuring that the head and prospective writers understood the roles of a content writer.

In discussions with prospective writers, I emphasized the following:

- A significant time commitment would be necessary
- The writing process was challenging
- They would be part of a team and not left alone to complete the package
- The skills they would need
- An outline of the development process, from design to use of the resource, and their roles

Any rewards for being a content writer were negotiated between the head of the school and the academic. Rewards varied depending on the academic's workload, needs, and wants. Examples of rewards include the writing time as a component of the academic's total workload hours and financial payment for completing the task outside of work hours.

My advice to project managers is to tell the truth about the time commitment necessary and the challenges to be overcome. Being a content writer is never easy, and teachers need to know this before they commit to joining a project team.

programmer usually spends most of the time writing programs and may work on a number of projects simultaneously.

The purpose of the following list of potential rewards for teachers who are content writers in flexible learning projects is to

- help teachers consider the rewards when they are deciding whether to be involved;
- assist teachers in negotiating conditions for their involvement; and
- to offer suggestions to project managers and heads of schools about the types of rewards and incentives that can be offered.

The rewards of being a content writer can include the following:

- A sense of helping students by using your expertise to develop resources
- Opportunities to reflect on and further develop your understanding of course concepts

- Continued development of your understanding of teaching and learning strategies
- An opportunity to develop your technology literacy in projects that use the latest technologies
- Development of your teaching portfolio and increased attractiveness to employers
- Ownership or joint ownership of the resource's copyright
- Time off from other duties, for example, fewer teaching or administrative activities
- Financial payment for writing the content outside of normal working hours

KEY POINTS

1. You do not have to choose between buying or developing learning resources. Both can be done.
2. The unique attraction of developing resources is that it allows students to "hear" their teachers' voices, to experience the teachers' thoughts, experiences, and interpretations.
3. Stakeholder meetings set the scope for a project. Make sure they are well planned, as the opportunity to get stakeholders to attend the same meeting is too rare to waste.
4. The more people who know about the project, the better. Listen to all advice and consider its merits.

Chapter 4

Educational and Design Foundations

A project is influenced by the educational beliefs of the team members. Constructivism is one theory of knowing that is consistent with flexible learning approaches. This theory provides theoretical foundations for a project.

The educational and design foundations on which a learning resource is developed consist of media-independent and media-dependent components. It is important that a project team adequately focus on media-independent issues, such as the writing of quality content and a course outline. The design of resources should be based on helping students answer the questions: Why am I using this resource? Where am I? Where can I go? What have I seen? How does this relate to my world? How can I determine if I understand? What do other people think?

OBJECTIVES

1. To describe a theory of knowledge called constructivism and its implications for the roles of students and teachers in a flexible learning environment
2. To emphasize the importance of focusing on the writing of quality content, irrespective of the media used, and to provide guidelines for the creation of a guidance document
3. To provide medium-independent advice about designing a learning resource so that students are encouraged and able to answer these questions:

   - Why am I using this resource?
   - Where am I?
   - Where can I go?
   - What have I seen?

- How does this relate to my world?
- How can I determine if I understand?
- What do other people think?

4. To provide guidance about writing a course outline document
5. To provide advice about using copyrighted work in a flexible learning resource, with an emphasis on the process of obtaining reproduction rights, and to discuss issues associated with claiming the copyright of a resource, and in particular what it means to say, "I hold the copyright"

TOPIC 4.1: INTRODUCTION

This chapter is addressed to content writers, project managers, and educational designers. The goal is to provide information that is useful regardless of the medium used and the amount of a course syllabus that a resource is being designed for.

Constructivism is a theory of knowledge that I believe is consistent with flexible learning. The foundations of this theory and its implications for the roles of teachers and students are examined in Topic 4.2. The remainder of the chapter is devoted to matters that are important for ensuring quality learning resources are developed.

- Topic 4.3 provides guidelines about writing quality content.
- Topic 4.4 includes educational guidelines about designing resources that help students answer the questions listed earlier.
- Topic 4.5 describes the contents of a course outline document and includes recommendations about writing such a document. Every course, regardless of its mix of on-campus and off-campus activities, needs a course outline.
- Topic 4.6 is devoted to the issue of copyright.

TOPIC 4.2: CONSTRUCTIVISM—
A THEORY OF KNOWLEDGE

What is constructivism? Although there is no one answer to this question, the following summarizes the constructivist theory to which I subscribe:

- "Knowledge is constructed in the mind of the learner" (Bodner, 1986, p. 873). Resources such as books, lecture notes, newspapers, Web sites, and videos contain information, not knowledge. As you use a resource, you do not absorb knowledge; instead you construct it.
- A person's knowledge is unique. It is not an exact reflection of an objective reality (von Glasersfeld, 1984, 1990; Wheatley, 1989; Bodner, 1986). There are similarities among people's understandings, but they are never exactly the same.
- Information is not transferred from person to person. Rather, information is transmitted, through resources, as signals. A person receives some of the transmitted signals.
- The process of knowledge construction involves the interaction of newly acquired information with the "characteristics of the person, such as existing knowledge, abilities and attitudes, which have their roots in experiences and in genetic inheritance, and the context in which the learning occurs" (White, 1988, p. ix).
- Prior knowledge influences a person's interpretation of information.
- If the information does not conflict with a person's current understanding, a process of assimilation occurs as no major conceptual revision is required (von Glasersfeld, 1990; Wittrock, 1985; Strike and Posner, 1985).
- If the information conflicts with a person's prior knowledge, one of three things occurs:
  a. the information will be ignored;
  b. knowledge will be constructed but considered as a separate entity from the prior knowledge; or
  c. a process of accommodation happens that involves the modification of the person's prior knowledge (von Glasersfeld, 1990; Wittrock, 1985; Strike and Posner, 1985).
- Learning is the process of developing understanding.

Implications of Constructivism for the Roles of Students and Teachers

Adopting a constructivist model of knowing affects how you see the roles of students and teachers. People do not necessarily perform

these roles automatically. To encourage them, it is necessary to create an appropriate learning and teaching environment.

The Roles of Students

The following are students' roles consistent with a constructivist outlook.

- Students recognize that they are responsible for their learning strategies. They recognize that to refine and expand their understandings, they need to be explorers seeking out information (Mitchell, 1993; Winn, 1991; Wheatley, 1989).
- Students accept that their understandings of a concept will evolve as they encounter information and reflect upon their understandings. They are willing to tell teachers when they are not satisfied with their understandings of a concept (Mitchell, 1993).

- Students discuss the validity of their understandings in small and large groups. They accept that people have different understandings of the same concept. They respect people's right to argue the validity of their understandings (Mitchell, 1993; Wheatley, 1989).
- Students acknowledge that learning is a complex task that
  a. involves relating new information to prior knowledge;
  b. requires time for reflection;
  c. is facilitated by being inquisitive and challenging oneself; and
  d. involves developing relationships between concepts (Mitchell, 1993).
- When attempting to answer questions, students do not give up if the answer is not immediately apparent. If their answers are incorrect, they seek out the reasons. Students can explain their answers (Mitchell, 1993).

The Roles of Teachers

To facilitate the students' roles, teachers fill the following roles:

- Teachers recognize that "the logical order of presentation of material in the mind of an expert is not always the best order of presentation so that a novice will learn the material" (Bodner, 1986, p. 877). They provide students with the opportunity to have significant control over their sequences of content (Jonassen, 1991).
- Teachers recognize that for some students an activity will lead to greater understandings of a concept, whereas for other students different activities will be required. Therefore, teachers provide a range of activities (Jonassen et al., 1993).
- Teachers attempt to gain an understanding of the prior knowledge of students so that they can make available activities that will challenge students' current understandings and require reflection and discussion (Jonassen et al., 1993; Wheatley, 1989).
- Teachers develop trust between themselves and students, and among students. By the establishment of trust, teachers are likely to be able to encourage students to tell them when they do not understand, and encourage small and large group discus-

sions in which students and teachers debate, and possibly modify, their understandings of concepts (Jonassen et al., 1993).

- Teachers encourage students to accept that people's views differ, and that questioning, answering, and being able to justify their answers are important elements of learning. Teachers
  a. answer questions at the time they are asked;
  b. ask many students for their answers before passing judgment; and
  c. ask students to justify their answers irrespective of whether they are right or wrong (Mitchell, 1993; Wheatley, 1989; Bodner, 1986).

- Teachers recognize that although they may have an understanding of the relationship of a topic to the syllabus, students have difficulty understanding the relationship. As Bodner (1986, p. 877) comments, "Students never know where you are going to be in a few weeks (or months); they have a hard enough time remembering where you have been." Therefore, teachers must ensure that they explain how information relates to recently discussed concepts as well as students' experiences outside the classroom (Jonassen et al., 1993; Cunningham, 1991; Wheatley, 1989).

Constructivism and Flexible Learning

If we accept that students are individuals, each with a different prior knowledge and each with different learning-style preferences, then our role as educators is to support this variety among students, that is, to offer a range of learning opportunities. Providing such choice is the key feature of a flexible learning environment. The development and maintenance of a teaching and learning environment that results in students being given a choice of learning opportunities, which use a variety of media, is called a flexible learning project.

A constructivist outlook underlies the advice I provide in this handbook. My goal is to help you develop teaching and learning environments that facilitate the "constructivist" roles of students and teachers.

TOPIC 4.3: ENSURING QUALITY CONTENT

Quality content is information that is accurate and relates to the sections of the course syllabus for which the learning resource is being developed. In Topic 1.4 a development model is presented that includes the writing of quality content. To this content a design is applied, in a production process, which results in a learning resource (Figure 1.1).

Quality content should be developed regardless of the media used in the learning resource. For example, a process to ensure quality content should be part of developing a print-based package, a CD-ROM, or a Web site. By seeing it as a process in its own right, there is less likelihood of the project team focusing on design and production to the detriment of the content. There is little point in developing learning resources that are based on a comprehensive design and production process if the content is not accurate and does not relate to the targeted sections of the course syllabus.

Figure 4.1 shows the process of ensuring quality content and the following list presents guidelines for developing it:

- *Develop a guidance document:* This is the crucial step in ensuring quality content.
- *Ensure content writers are knowledgeable about the course:* It is better to have a number of content writers who each focus on the syllabus sections they are experts in than to have one writer who struggles.
- *Use peer reviewers:* To help ensure the accuracy and appropriateness of information, use peer reviewers.
- *Think content before design:* Resist the temptation to think too much about design issues before ensuring the information is quality content.
- *Use paper:* Regardless of the media that will be used in the resource, the content writer should develop the underlying content in a printable form. Paper is portable and annotations are easy to make. The act of writing, or typing, can encourage reflection and careful construction of information.

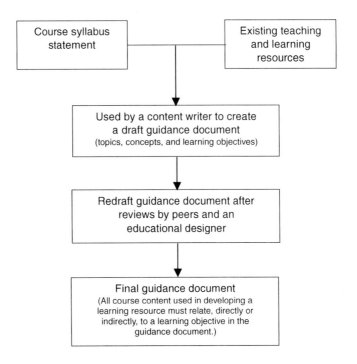

FIGURE 4.1. The Process of Ensuring Quality Content

Writing a Guidance Document

A ***guidance document*** *lists the topics, concepts, and learning objectives for which a learning resource is developed.*

The objectives of writing a guidance document are:

- to help content writers identify the parts of the course syllabus for which a learning resource will be developed; and
- to keep the development process focused on the creation of a resource that will help students achieve the learning objectives.

Table 4.1 is an extract from a guidance document. The size of a guidance document depends on the amount of a syllabus that a learn-

TABLE 4.1. Guidance Document Extract from a Twelve-Unit Course About Teaching Online to be Studied by Teachers As Part of Their Professional Development Activities—Unit Title: Computer-Mediated Contact (CMC): Staying in Touch with Students

Topic	Concepts and Issues	Learning Objective(s)
Introduction to CMC	What is CMC? Categories of CMC—synchronous and asynchronous, with an emphasis on the asynchronous types: e-mail, Web forums, and Listservs.	Demonstrate an understanding of what CMC is by describing common synchronous and asynchronous tools.
The advantages and challenges of CMC	CMC is not limited to flexible/distance education. It has uses in weekly on-campus environments. Six main advantages for students: 1. Able to receive information to help develop understanding. 2. Discuss life experiences related to the course. 3. Gain experience in offering ideas, receiving feedback, and modifying ideas. 4. Able to explore concepts to a deeper level than required. 5. Asynchronous forms allow time for reflection before posting a message. 6. The isolation common to flexible learning can be reduced. CMC helps teachers in at least four ways: 1. As frequently asked questions (FAQs) databases. 2. Helps in developing understanding of the students—professional and personal. 3. E-mail contact supports personalized teacher-student contact. 4. Teachers can refine their understandings of course concepts.	Describe two situations in which CMC could be used in a course that involves weekly on-campus lectures and tutorials. Demonstrate an understanding of the advantages of CMC for flexible learning students and teachers, with reference to a course you teach.

61

TABLE 4.1 (continued)

Topic	Concepts and Issues	Learning Objective(s)
	Seven challenges for teachers and students: 1. Very different from face-to-face teaching with lack of visual and verbal clues. 2. Need to be able to analyze messages and phrase questions. 3. Asynchronous anxiety—"has the teacher received my e-mail"—is common. 4. Time management skills are needed. 5. Financial costs. 6. People need to post messages; otherwise there is much unrealized potential. 7. Have to learn e-mail and Web browser applications.	List the seven challenges for teachers and students of CMC environments, and describe ways in which adverse effects can be minimized.
The roles of teachers	Best practices for teachers: • Tell students explicitly how you will be involved. • Practice what you preach. • Integrate CMC into the curriculum. • Be able to help students with standard technical issues. The teacher as moderator: Explain what moderation is and that being a censor is a minor part. Teaching strategies: • Define what they are. • Explain that the most appropriate strategies depend on the type of course. • Alert to argument; any problems; assessment; brainstorm; critique an article; cross-fertilization; debate; false statement; guests; hot seat; online poll; reactivation; revisit; rewording an ignored posting; small group work; student moderator; target a Web site; weaving; Web site comparisons.	Write a statement for students describing how you will use a CMC environment and your expectations of students. For a course that you teach, list five CMC teaching strategies. For each strategy, provide an example of how you would apply it.

		Write a student CMC training and support plan for a course you teach.
	Social strategies: • Define what they are. • Chatter; an online conversation not a publication; observers, rudeness; situated learning; we are all learning; who are you; who's who. Managerial strategies: • Define what they are. • Check locations; going away; no lecturing; start with guidelines about contributing; take breaks; you are the boss, not the computer. • Netiquette: Explicitly state what is acceptable and unacceptable behavior, and the penalties for inappropriate messages.	
Training and support	Define training and support. For teachers—technical and educational issues: • Importance of training early enough and practicing on the course Web site • Continuous support, including a person in the school What the students need: • Both technical and educational issues • Training in the first weeks of the semester and support throughout	

ing resource is being designed for. For example, Table 4.1 represents one-twelfth of the guidance document created for a "teaching online" course. Guidelines for writing such a document include the following:

- Use three columns: topic, concepts and issues, and learning objective(s).
- The content writer completes the document with reference to the appropriate sections of the course syllabus.
- Often the course syllabus statement is not detailed enough, and the writer needs to also use existing course teaching and learning resources.
- Ideally, the learning objectives are written addressing the students. For example: "After studying this unit, you should be able to achieve the following objectives."
- Completing the guidance document takes time. The writer needs to consider whether parts of the syllabus should be changed and give particular attention to those parts that students often have difficulty understanding.
- The educational designer and the peer reviewers consider drafts of the guidance document and provide feedback to the content writer (see Exhibit 4.1).

EXHIBIT 4.1. The Challenges of Writing a Guidance Document

For each of the courses in the HTM Project, the first stage in developing a learning resource was to write a guidance document. As the educational designer I provided the content writers with guidelines and examples.

Understandably, content writers found it challenging to think of the entire course structure. The need to think and plan ahead meant that the first activity for many writers was to review the existing curriculum, including any existing teaching and learning resources. On average three drafts of a guidance document were written before all participants—the writer, the peer reviewers, and educational designer—were satisfied. However, this did not mean that the document could not be altered. Often a document was modified as the course notes were written. Some modification is to be expected, as it is only when immersed in the writing process that it becomes evident to writers and reviewers that certain concepts belong in different topics, that others should be deleted, and some new concepts should be introduced.

TOPIC 4.4: EDUCATIONAL DESIGN GUIDELINES FOR LEARNING RESOURCES

As shown in Figure 1.1, a learning resource is developed by applying a design to quality content. A learning resource is something that students use to help them develop their understandings of course content. It is a source of information. Examples of learning resources are teachers, fellow students, colleagues, libraries, Web sites, notes, CD-ROMs, videos, television programs, newspapers, and textbooks.

A design has media-independent and media-dependent parts. In this topic, the media-independent components are discussed. The aim is to provide guidelines about what makes an effective learning resource. The information in this topic will be of particular interest to content writers and educational designers, as it focuses on the educational aspects of design.

A design is a balance between rules and creativity. The creativity of the project team should not be excessively constrained by design rules. For example, explicitly listing learning objectives is a common rule. However, there are situations in which rules should not be followed. For example, in a computer simulation the objectives may be implied through actions, rather than being explicitly described.

Before presenting the design guidelines, I want to emphasize that not every learning activity has to involve students using at least one of their five senses—sight, smell, touch, hearing, and taste. An activity can only involve thinking and still be good. Although interactive activities play an important role in helping students, the focus on electronic resources, such as Web sites and computer-based simulations, has resulted in the promotion of "doing" over "thinking." A theme throughout this handbook is balance. In most situations, variety is what is needed.

A design should help students answer the following questions.

Why Am I Using This Resource?

Students should be provided with specific reasons why they are using a resource, rather than a general statement telling them that it will help them understand the course. A learning resource usually consists of a number of sections, which are called units. Each unit can have an introduction in which the concepts discussed are introduced and the unit's relationship to the rest of the resource explained.

Another way of helping students is to have a list of unit learning objectives. The objectives need to be written so that

- before they study a unit, students are able to read the objectives and determine the extent to which they already understand the content;
- as students study, the objectives act as a target helping to keep them oriented, focused, and motivated; and
- once students have studied the content, they are able to determine whether they can achieve the objectives.

Learning objectives should be written as part of the guidance document (Topic 4.3). Writing objectives is not easy and is best done as a team effort including the content writer, the educational designer, and the peer reviewers.

Race (1993) contains detailed information about writing learning objectives, which he calls learning outcomes. The following guidelines are an introduction to writing learning objectives:

- Write the learning objectives as part of the guidance document and use them to guide the development of quality content.
- Once the content is written, reconsider the objectives. You may need to modify them to make sure the objectives and content match.
- Address the students and use a nonacademic style of writing. Instead of saying, "The student will be competent in the following objectives once the unit is completed," write, "After studying this unit, you should be able to achieve the following objectives."
- The meaning of an objective must be clear. It has to state what students need to be able to achieve and how they are expected to demonstrate their understandings. Use words that have definite meanings rather than vague words such as *understand* and *know*. Instead of saying, "Demonstrate an understanding of the essential characteristics of service," write, "List and describe the three essential characteristics of service, relating these (1) to the theory that consumers typically rely on 'experience properties' when evaluating service quality; and (2) to the notion that cus-

tomers are the sole judges of service quality." Instead of saying, "List common barriers to improving service quality and briefly describe the principles and strategies for implementing organizational changes to remove these obstacles," write, "List common barriers to improving service quality and briefly describe the four key principles and four key strategies for implementing organizational change to remove these obstacles."

• Include objectives that involve students relating course concepts to their everyday lives. Instead of saying, "Illustrate the diversity of service provision within the hospitality industry," write, "Illustrate, by using Hong Kong examples, the diversity of service provision within the local hospitality industry."

Where Am I? Where Can I Go? What Have I Seen?

To support choice, the design of a resource should be such that a student can answer these questions at any time. Designing so that the three questions can always be answered is a media-specific issue. In

Topic 6.4 the questions are considered in relation to print-based resources. In Topic 7.5 they are considered in relation to Web sites.

How Does This Relate to My World?

To help students understand course concepts, efforts should be made to relate content to their professional and personal lives. That is, content should be contextualized.

---

*Content is **contextualized** when it is related to the everyday activities of students and the worlds in which they live.*

Unfortunately, many flexible learning courses contain inadequately contextualized learning resources. Reasons for this include

- the use of exactly the same resources for all students regardless of where they live; and
- a lack of awareness of the students' worlds.

To some extent, a lack of contextualization is understandable in situations in which a course is being completed by a group of students that are living in many different countries. For example, a group may consist of twenty students from five countries. In such a situation an institution cannot be expected to produce a version of the resource contextualized to each country. However, exercises can be included that encourage students to contextualize the concepts themselves. Such exercises need to be written using general language, rather than mentioning specific situations, and ask students to observe their environments. For example, a course about front-of-house service in hotels can include a topic about the roles and skills of front-of-house personnel. An exercise can be included that requires students to visit some of their local hotels and sit briefly in the foyer watching the front-of-house operations.

However, in most cases students are not widely dispersed. For example, as a Hong Kong student I would expect a Hong Kong institution to ensure that resources are contextualized. Equally, I would expect an overseas institution to contextualize their resources if I were one of twenty Hong Kong students studying the course. For example, it would be disappointing, and possibly confusing, if the operation of a sheep station was used to illustrate the importance of water conservation techniques when the example of conserving water in a Hong Kong business would be more appropriate (see Exhibit 4.2).

The content writer and the educational designer are primarily responsible for contextualization. Media-specific techniques are de-

EXHIBIT 4.2. Contextualization: An Expatriate in Hong Kong

As an educational designer in the HTM Project, I advocated that learning resources should reflect the Hong Kong environment in which students lived.

Why Was Contextualization Emphasized in the HTM Project?

- Hotel and tourism management is an applied social science. Therefore, understanding the application of concepts in the real world, including the hospitality industry, is important.
- The hotel and tourism sector is a major part of the Hong Kong economy. Therefore, there were many opportunities to use local examples and case studies.
- Many of the resources students used were contextualized for the United States or British environments. With the development of the print-based packages, the opportunity existed to offer more localized explanations.

How Was Contextualization Achieved?

- I lived in Hong Kong for the first two years of the project as an expatriate Anglo-Saxon Australian. My awareness of cultural values, colloquial language, and second-language issues was minimal. Therefore, it was important that I encouraged other team members to consider contextualization issues.
- Content writers and peer reviewers, for whom Cantonese was their first language, played an important part in ensuring the materials, written in English, were designed to cater to the challenges people face when reading material in a second language.
- In a few cases the content writer for a package was a non-Cantonese-speaking expatriate. In these situations I sought the views of local Cantonese-speaking staff about the appropriateness of examples.
- The HTM Project benefited from the project assistant having recently graduated from the school and her everyday experiences being closer to those of the students than other team members.

scribed in Topic 6.4 for print resources and Topic 7.5 for Web-based resources. As you consider the following guidelines, remember that contextualization is an issue not only for students living in other countries but also for local students.

- *Think of the five senses.* Having an awareness of what students see, hear, taste, feel, and smell can help you think of examples they will relate to.
- *Remember that the way you live may not be similar to the way students live.* For example, comparing the challenges in planning a restaurant to maximize the number of patrons to planning a three-bedroom apartment is unlikely to be an appropriate comparison for an undergraduate student who rents a one-bedroom apartment with three colleagues. Even though you may live in the same city or suburb as the students, contextualization can be a challenge. For example, how many students visit the restaurants you visit?
- *Ask a local person to think of examples.* If you are adapting a learning resource for use in a different context than the original one, ask a local person to review the material and suggest replacements for examples that are not appropriate.
- *Ask students for examples of concepts being applied in their everyday environments.*
- *Be aware of cultural values.* In situations in which you are developing a resource for use in a culture different than yours, it can be a challenge to account for cultural factors. Ask a local teacher to evaluate the resource.
- *Do not use colloquial language and jokes unless you are certain students will understand.*
- *Visit the country.* If you are developing resources for students living in a country different from yours, visit the country. An alternative is to read travel books.

How Can I Determine If I Understand?

The role of learning objectives in helping students focus on understanding course content has already been described in the section Why Am I Using This Resource?

To help students determine whether they can achieve an objective, assessment opportunities can be provided. These can take the form of

- formal assessment, such as assignments and examinations that contribute to a student's course grade; or
- self-exercises.

A *self-exercise:*

- *is a question or task, and a response that consists of an answer and ideally an explanation; and*
- *is designed to help students self-evaluate their understandings of recently considered content.*

When designing self-exercises, content writers should keep a number of issues in mind:

- The main purpose of a self-exercise is to help students self-evaluate their understandings. It is not intended to give them practice at answering exam-type questions. The problem in using exam-type questions is that they usually require more time than a self-exercise should take to complete. Also, self-assessing the quality of a short answer or essay is not easy. Assignments are a more appropriate place for questions requiring detailed written answers.
- It can be tempting to use self-exercises to evaluate the progress of students. This is done by releasing responses to the exercises only after students have sent the teacher their attempts. This is inconsistent with the purpose of a self-exercise.
- It is important to provide variety in the exercise types. For example, common types in print-based resources are diagram completion, short answer, matching, and check the box.
- The media used in the learning resource influence the types of self-exercises provided. For example, a Web site can include a simulation exercise that involves students altering variable values and instantaneously seeing the effects. With a print-based resource, such simulations are more difficult to provide.
- The nature of the course influences the types of self-exercises. For example, a financial management course is suited to exercises that involve filling in spaces on balance sheets. A strategic marketing course, which includes more competing theories and models, is more suited to short-answer exercises.

The following list describes the foundations of a good self-exercise:

- The question or task has the following characteristics.
  a. It is explained in concise and clear language.
  b. When a written answer is expected, there is an indication of how many words should be written.
  c. In a complex exercise, an answer to one part is included to help students know what to do.
- The response has the following characteristics.
  a. An answer is always provided. In cases that have no single correct answer, a "model" answer is included.
  b. Students need to be able to quickly check their attempts. Therefore, the answer is provided before any explanations, and a format similar to the question is used. For example, in a check-the-box exercise, the table used in the question is reproduced in the answer, with the correct boxes checked.
  c. An explanation follows the answer. Its focus is on explaining the parts of the question or task that students would be likely to have difficulties in answering.
- The focus is on helping students test their understandings of content that the teacher believes they are likely to find challenging.
- The question or task immediately follows the presentation of the related content.
- Completing an exercise should take between five and fifteen minutes.
- The difficulty level of exercises varies throughout the resource.

What Do Other People Think?

Students should be encouraged to discuss course content with their fellow students and the teacher. Such communication can help develop their understandings. Also, discussions can help students realize that people can have different, yet valid, understandings of concepts and events.

Activities can be included in learning resources to help students find out what other people think. These media-specific methods are discussed in Topic 6.4 for print resources, and Topic 7.5 and Topic 8.3 for Internet-based resources.

TOPIC 4.5: WRITING A COURSE OUTLINE

A **course outline** *is a document that introduces students to the teacher, the content, the requirements for successful course completion, and the learning resources.*

Every course should have an outline, regardless of the teaching and learning environment. Such a document helps to orient students, describing what they can expect and what is expected of them. In flexible learning environments, the document needs to be very comprehensive. Students may attend school on campus infrequently, if at all. In this topic, the structure of a course outline is described and guidelines for writing one provided.

A course outline should contain the following sections:

- *Important notes:* These explain what students need to do in the first week of study. For example, send an e-mail to the teacher so that an accurate list of addresses is created.
- *About your teacher:* Introduce the teacher, including a description of academic and industry-based experiences.
- *About the course:* The goals and objectives of the course are presented.
- *Why study this course?* The benefits of the course are described, with an emphasis on its role in helping students meet industry needs.
- *The learning resources:* A list of the learning resources is included, with the core resources distinguished from the supplementary resources.
- *How do I study this course?* The semester structure, indicating events such as on-campus sessions, is described, and a suggested study schedule is included.
- *How to use the learning resources:* Features of the learning resources are described, with emphasis given to those that students may find different from previous courses.
- *Assessment:* The assessment structure is explained, including the number of assessable items, when assignments are due, and their values. The marking scheme is explained and assignment cover sheets provided.

The following are guidelines about the process of writing a course outline.

- *Use a personal and approachable writing style.* An outline is usually the first document a student reads. Personalize the outline by describing your experiences and reassuring students that although the course will be challenging, they will be supported.
- *Write the outline last.* The course outline is written after all resources have been developed, purchased, or both. This helps ensure that the document accurately describes the teaching and learning environment.
- *Use the first language for essential information.* It is essential that students understand some parts of the document, such as assignment descriptions and submission procedures. If the outline is written in a language other than the students' primary language, include the essential information in both languages.
- *Be comprehensive and succinct.* Writing a course outline is not easy. You can expect to go through many drafts as you aim to include all the important information yet make sure the document is concise.
- *If there is a face-to-face meeting, discuss the outline.* If an on-campus class is held at the start of semester, key parts of the document, such as the suggested study schedule and assignment details, should be explained.
- *Maintain the document.* Every semester the document will need maintenance, as it contains time-dependent information, such as assignment and study dates.

TOPIC 4.6: COPYRIGHT

Consider the following scenario. You are a content writer thinking about including a diagram from a journal article in a flexible learning resource. Many questions need answers: Why do you want to include the diagram? Are there alternatives, such as your own description or diagram? Do you need to obtain permission to reproduce the diagram? If so, how do you obtain permission?

Now consider a second scenario. As a content writer, you have been part of a team developing a course Web site. Who has copyright of the content, the design, and the programming code? What does it mean to hold the copyright? How much effort should be made to enforce copyright? What are the alternatives to standard copyright licenses?

This topic aims to help content writers, project managers, and educational designers answer these questions. The advice relates to flexible learning environments in educational institutions and is not a replacement for consulting experts.

Copyright *is "the exclusive right, granted by law for a certain number of years, to make and dispose of copies of, and otherwise to control, a literary, musical, dramatic, or artistic work" (Macquarie Dictionary, 1998).*

A work is an expression of an idea, as distinct from the idea itself, and "the principle of copyright is not to protect an idea, but rather, the specific expression of that idea" (Downes, 2003).

Using Copyrighted Work in a Flexible Learning Resource

The following list contains key guidelines and considerations about using copyrighted works in a flexible learning resource:

- The project manager is responsible for ensuring team members are aware of their responsibilities and the procedures associated with using copyrighted work.
- Seek the advice of experts, such as the staff of the institution's teaching and learning department and librarians.
- Study the copyright license. You may be able to use the work without having to obtain specific permission to reproduce it, as long as you meet the stipulated conditions.
- Adopt an "if in doubt apply for reproduction permission" approach to copyright.
- Obtaining reproduction permissions is time-consuming and can be expensive. Therefore, be sure that the work is needed and an alternative does not exist. For example, a computer programmer wanting to use copyrighted code needs to be sure that alternative code (that may be less elegant but just as effective) cannot be written. A content writer needs to be convinced that a diagram will help students understand a concept. A Web designer want-

ing to use a copyrighted photo of a city may be able to find a royalty-free alternative.

- Start the process of seeking reproduction rights early in the resource production process. It can take months to receive replies to your requests.
- In general, use is granted under strict conditions. For example, reproduction permission can be granted for the use of a work only in a specified course and year, in a specified medium, and for a set number of copies.
- In general, the more prestigious and commercial the source, the greater the reproduction fee. Works from textbooks have higher fees than similar works from journal articles.

Is It Always Necessary to Request Reproduction Permission?

Whether reproduction permission needs to be sought depends on a multitude of interrelated factors that are context-dependent. Therefore, I cannot offer a definitive answer to this question. Instead, here are some of the factors that will determine the answer:

- Fair-use principles, especially as applied to resources used by educational institutions, may allow a work to be used without specific permission from the copyright holder, as long as conditions such as acknowledgment of the source are met.
- The license conditions for a work may allow its use without specific reproduction permission. For example:
  a. An *attribution* license allows the copying, distribution, display, and performance of a work, and works derived from it, as long as the copyright holder is acknowledged.
  b. A *noncommercial* license is similar to an attribution license, but limits your use of a work to noncommercial purposes.
  c. A *no derivative works* license is similar to an attribution license, but does not permit the creation of derivative works.
- The medium, or media, in which you intend to include a work may influence whether specific permission needs to be obtained. For example, while some academic journals permit the inclusion of extracts in print-based packages, as long as acknowledgment is included, they usually prohibit such use in Web sites without granting specific permission.

- The degree to which a work you have created is derived, that is, adapted, from a copyrighted work influences whether specific reproduction permission is required. The questions you need to ask yourself are many, such as: To what extent did you take a copyrighted diagram and make alterations? What is the extent of those alterations? Did you draw your own diagram using the original as a source of inspiration?

The Process of Obtaining Reproduction Rights

Obtaining the right to reproduce or adapt a work takes time. Letters need to be sent early in the resource production process. This section focuses on obtaining rights for works that content writers commonly want to include in a flexible learning resource. Figure 4.2 summarizes the process of seeking reproduction rights.

Two components of the process of seeking reproduction rights illustrated in Figure 4.2 are worth more detailed examination. These are the reproduction request form, completed by the content writer, and the request letter, created by the educational designer or project assistant.

In the reproduction request form the writer specifies

- the type of item, for example an entire article, an extract from an article or textbook, a photo, a diagram, or a table;
- where in the resource the item will appear;
- the medium(s) of the resource;
- whether an exact copy will be used or an adaptation, that is, derivation, of the item; and
- the contact details of the copyright holder.

Also, a copy of the item is attached to the request form.

The objective in writing the request letter is to provide concise details of the item and how it will be used. Many copyright holders are major publishers who receive thousands of requests. Your goal is to help the publisher quickly deal with the request. The request letter, written on institutional letterhead paper and attached to a copy of the item, includes

- the details provided on the reproduction request form;
- the maximum number of copies per year;

- fax and e-mail details, as well as the institution's postal address to encourage a prompt reply;
- a request for one-time reproduction rights; and
- a return slip that the copyright holder can sign and return.

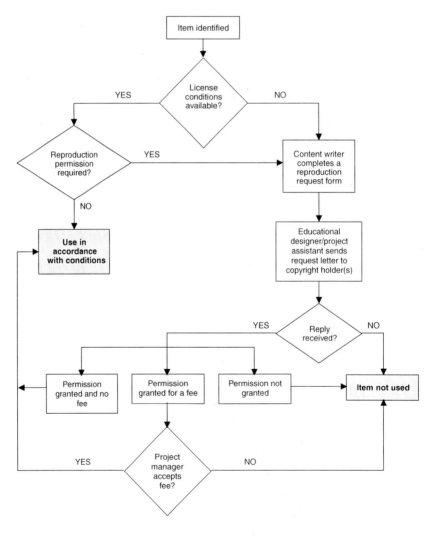

FIGURE 4.2. Obtaining Reproduction Rights

If one-time rights are granted, it allows the use of the item every year, in accordance with the conditions stipulated, without having to reapply for permission. Special attention needs to be paid to items that are themselves derived from other works. In this situation, request letters need to be sent to the copyright holders of the original and the derived items.

Copyright of a Flexible Learning Resource

A work is copyrighted once it is created. There is no need to place the copyright symbol on the work or to state the fact. However, placing a copyright symbol on a work, expressing copyright ownership in words, and registering the copyright with a government agency will help prospective users contact you and may deter people from breaking copyright.

Who Owns the Copyright of a Work and What Does It Mean?

Ownership of the copyright of flexible learning resources developed by people employed by educational institutions is a contentious area; disagreements between staff and institutions are common. Many of the disagreements relate to the differing perspectives of people. It is common for an institution to treat a resource, such as a paper-based package, as a product with a competitive value, while the teacher who wrote the content treats it as personal intellectual property.

Determining the holders of the copyright depends on how the resource was created, the policies of the institution, and the laws of the country. In determining ownership, you need to consider questions such as the following:

- To what extent was the resource the result of a team effort? For example, as a content writer you may have been involved in the creation of a course Web site. However, a Web designer also worked full-time on the project and an educational designer assisted in the creation of self-assessment exercises.
- Were people employed specifically to work on developing the resource, or was their involvement in addition to their core duties? For example, a consultant employed as a content writer may have difficulty claiming copyright of the intellectual prop-

erty, as the writer is defined as a person hired by an institution to complete a task for which payment is received. This compares to the situation many teachers find themselves in, where they are employed as academics, with research and teaching responsibilities, and are also required to develop learning resources.

• To what degree was the work original?

I recommend that before people expend time and energy arguing among themselves and with their institution about copyright ownership, they think about two issues. First, what does it mean to claim copyright? Second, what is the reason for holding and enforcing copyright? In relation to the first question, Downes (2003) wrote, "Though original authorship is frequently claimed, it is seldom, if ever the case." For example, consider a teacher claiming copyright over the content of a 300-page flexible learning package. By claiming copyright, the teacher is asserting that every expression of an idea that is not attributed to someone else is unique and the result of original thinking by the teacher. This is a significant claim. It may be true. However, it is worth thinking about just what claiming copyright means before a teacher, a Web designer, an educational designer, or institution claims possession of a resource.

Why Hold Copyright?

Wanting the copyright of a resource is not always about restricting copying and earning sufficient royalties to retire at age thirty! Instead a person may want to ensure that open access to a resource is maintained. For example, although an institution may want to limit access to a package, a teacher may want to encourage the distribution of the resource by claiming copyright and placing a license on it such as an attribution license or noncommercial license.

Regardless of the reasons why people, or institutions, hold the copyright of a resource, they need to be able to enforce it. However, enforcement is problematical. If a person wants to ensure absolute enforcement, then there must be only one copy of the resource and it must be in the person's possession all the time. This is unrealistic and therefore a balance must be achieved between enforcement and use. In deciding the degree of enforcement, issues such as the following need to be considered:

- Enforcement can adversely affect attempts to maximize the return on investment (Topic 1.2).
- Enforcement can be time-consuming and expensive.
- In what situations would legal action be taken? For example, would you pursue a student at your institution who copied a package as vigorously as you would pursue another institution that copied significant sections of a package?

KEY POINTS

1. If you are a content writer or educational designer, keep reminding yourself of the importance of developing content that is accurate and relates to the course syllabus. Quality content is the foundation on which quality resources are developed.
2. As you design a learning resource, remind yourself of the questions students ask. Do not forget that the customers are the students, and a resource is designed to satisfy their needs and wants.
3. Before using a real-world example to describe a concept, ask yourself, "Is this an example that many students will relate to?"

Chapter 5

Media Foundations

Regardless of the media used in offering students a range of learning resources, it is important that an institution values the irreplaceable role of teachers in a flexible learning environment.

Although the needs and wants of students and the technology available to them are the main factors that guide the determination of the media used, other factors associated with the teachers, the institution, and the nature of the course should be considered. In most situations, using more than one medium is best. The complexity and uniqueness of the learning process means that students react differently to different media at different stages of the development of their understandings.

OBJECTIVES

1. To emphasize the irreplaceable role of teachers in a flexible learning environment, because learning resources can only support, not replace, a teacher in helping students learn
2. To explain that the primary determinants of the media used for learning resources should be the needs and wants of students, and the technology available to them
3. To make project team members aware of teacher-, institution-, and course-related issues that can influence decisions about the media used for learning resources
4. To advocate the development of teaching and learning environments that provide a range of learning opportunities using a variety of media

TOPIC 5.1: INTRODUCTION

This chapter will be of interest to people involved in the initial stages of developing flexible learning resources. Deciding which media to use for learning resources involves more than just thinking about the advantages and disadvantages of particular media. It also involves consideration of

- students' needs, wants, and access to technology;
- teachers' needs and wants;
- institutional factors; and
- the characteristics of the course.

These are the issues considered in this chapter. The advantages and disadvantages of particular media are described in Chapters 6 to 9.

The words *medium* and *technology* mean different things to different people. This can result in confusion among project team members. Therefore, it is important that all members are aware of what the words mean in the context of the project.

A ***medium*** *is a method of distributing information. A medium does not exist without content.*

A ***technology*** *is a physical apparatus.*

Postman (1987) writes, "a technology is to a medium as the brain is to the mind. . . . A technology . . . is merely a machine. A medium is the social and intellectual environment a machine creates" (p. 86).

The definition of technology used in this handbook is more encompassing than that in many flexible learning books, which tend to restrict the definition to computers and the Internet. These are not the only examples of technology. Items such as pencils and paper also qualify.

A learning resource is a medium, that is, a method of distributing information. For example, a library contains information using a variety of media, such as books, videotapes, newspapers, and CD-ROMs. A textbook is a medium. A teacher is a medium.

A television can be used to explain the difference between a technology and a medium. A television that is turned off is a technology. A television that is turned on is a medium.

Although most of this chapter is addressed to content writers and educational designers, I recommend that project managers also read it. In order to be able to communicate with team members and plan, a project manager needs an awareness of media selection issues:

- Topic 5.2 emphasizes the essential position of teachers in providing quality learning environments.
- Topics 5.3 and 5.4 focus on factors to consider when choosing the media used in learning resources. Rarely is the decision based on one factor. Instead it is a multifactorial situation, with issues relating to students given more importance.
- In Topic 5.5 I advocate that as educationalists we should aim to create learning environments that involve media, instead of only one medium.

TOPIC 5.2: THE TEACHER IS ESSENTIAL

Dunkin (1987) defines pedagogy as "the art and science of teaching. It concerns the knowledge and skills that practitioners of the profession of teaching employ in performing their duties of facilitating desired learnings in others" (p. 319).

This definition of teaching as an art and a science is consistent with the belief that quality teaching cannot be formulaic. It cannot be divorced from the artist, and the artist is the teacher. Often the development of a flexible learning environment is seen as an attempt to reduce the roles of teachers and replace them with paper packages and Web sites. However, I have yet to meet students who want less contact with teachers. Therefore, I advocate that any flexible learning environment must include opportunities for teacher and student interaction. While recognizing the constraints of an environment, you should maximize the opportunities for such contact (Exhibit 5.1). For example, consider the following scenarios:

- In a course completed by students living in other countries, there should, at a minimum, be e-mail and phone communication with the teacher, and a local tutor regularly available for face-to-face discussions. Ideally, the teacher should visit the students for a few days of intensive contact. It is the student's choice whether to use these opportunities.

• In a course completed by students that live within 100 miles of the institution, there should, at a minimum, be e-mail and phone communication with the teacher and regular opportunities to meet face-to-face. It is the student's choice whether to use these opportunities.

Teachers are essential in flexible learning projects not only as content writers. They are also essential as teachers. The development of resources such as print packages (Chapter 6) and Web sites (Chapter 7) as core learning resources can help teachers reduce their role of being information providers and increase the time they devote to being information advisors—that is, people who help students make sense of information, taking into account each student's needs and wants.

EXHIBIT 5.1. E-Mail Access

In the HTM Project I recommended that teachers send a weekly e-mail and encouraged students to use e-mail to communicate with them.

Initially some teachers were reluctant. They argued that not all students had an e-mail address or regularly checked their e-mail accounts. In my counterargument I emphasized the following:

• The Hong Kong Internet infrastructure was well developed.
• For students who did not have adequate home, work, or on-campus access, there were many Internet cafés.
• E-mail was a supplementary resource, not a core resource essential to a student's success.

Although e-mail became a standard means of communication between teachers and students, it was necessary to initially force the issue. One of the roles of an educational designer is to encourage consideration of new teaching and learning aids. You have to balance the wants of teachers and students with the need to force consideration of new technology.

TOPIC 5.3: DETERMINING THE NEEDS, WANTS, AND TECHNOLOGY ACCESS OF STUDENTS

Before deciding which media to use for learning resources, content writers and educational designers have to develop their understandings of

- the course curriculum, including the syllabus;
- common student difficulties in understanding the syllabus; and
- the world in which students live.

Developing this understanding is part of identifying, and then satisfying, the needs and wants of students. Guidelines for determining the needs and wants of students include the following:

- *Develop an understanding of the curriculum, especially the course syllabus.* While a content writer must have an excellent understanding of the syllabus, it is important that the educational designer has at least an awareness of the course. A designer cannot develop learning opportunities without a basic understanding of the content.
- *Identify student difficulties and potential remedies.* Ideally, the content writer will have taught the course before. Therefore, the writer will have an understanding of which parts of the syllabus students are likely to find challenging. The educational literature and the opinions of other teachers should also be considered.
- *Talk to students.* Talking to students can offer insights into their needs and wants. However, in some cultures it is difficult for such discussions to occur. Therefore, also consider talking to past students. They can be less hesitant in expressing what their needs and wants were.
- *Remember that your world is not the students' world.* What you perceive as needs or wants can be vastly different from students' perceptions.

When determining the needs and wants of students, it is important to remember two points. First, students are not necessarily aware of all their needs. For example, students are not aware of all the content

they need to understand before they start the course. Second, not all the wants of students should be satisfied. For example, some only want information that relates strongly to the examination questions. A teaching and learning environment should help students satisfy needs and wants that are consistent with the educational philosophy of the teacher and the institution.

Students' Access to Technology

The project team needs to be aware of the types of technology that students have access to and the extent to which they are familiar with using the technology. For example, it would be unethical to develop a Web site for use as a core learning resource if not all students have adequate access to the Internet. Before choosing the media that will be used, certain issues need to be considered:

- *Are you developing a core or supplementary resource?* If you are developing a core learning resource, ensure that all students have adequate access to the technology. This access may be on campus, at home, or both. It depends on the extent to which students are expected to attend on-campus classes.

- *Do not overestimate the technology literacy of students.* People often say, "Those younger generations are so technology literate, nothing is beyond them!" This is not always true. Age is not necessarily a good predictor of technology literacy. It is one of many factors to take into account.
- *Remember that your world is not the students' world.* The technology you can access may be different than that of students. For example, Internet access in your office may be a lot faster than that of a student working at home or in an Internet café. Students most likely live in a social environment different from yours. You may have a private home study, while some students live in shared accommodations with minimal private space. In such an environment, using a computer for long periods of time may be difficult.
- *Ask students.* Conduct surveys and interviews with past and present students. Do not base decisions only on the results of general population surveys, which describe the access situation across a wide spectrum of people.
- *Think creatively about how to cater to students who do not have adequate access to the technology.* Just because some students do not have adequate access to a technology does not mean that others cannot use a resource. In such situations, the teacher needs to explore alternative ways of providing the information. For example, a teacher may distribute a weekly e-mail. However, a few students may not be able to access the Internet, and instead a paper copy is sent to them.

The most appropriate medium (or media) to use in a learning resource is not necessarily based on the latest technology. For example, a print resource may be most appropriate considering the needs, wants, and technology of students, teachers, and the institution. Some people criticize the use of "old" technology. However, helping students does not automatically mean the latest technology has to be used. Often when developing resources I tell a story I heard while attending a conference on technology in education, as a reminder of the usefulness of older technology. The presenter described how she was using radio to transmit information to students in Mongolia. When visiting the students' communities, she found that this was the most common form of technology. She was using a technology consistent with the students' environment. However, after her presentation, the focus of many people's comments was on how to "upgrade" the students to computers.

TOPIC 5.4: SECONDARY DETERMINANTS— TEACHER, INSTITUTION, AND COURSE FACTORS

Although the needs, wants, and technology of students are the main factors to consider when choosing the media for learning resources, the teachers, the institution, and the characteristics of the course should also be considered.

Teacher-Related Factors

Teachers who are asked to be involved as content writers in the development and use of flexible learning resources should think about the following personal factors when determining which media to use in learning resources:

- *Professional and career development:* Being involved with projects that involve the latest technology can be advantageous. Usually an institution's management actively encourages such projects and values those involved.
- *A teacher's technology literacy:* Ideally, being involved in a project will provide you with professional development opportunities. For example, you may learn how to use new computer software. However, your primary roles are as a teacher and a content writer. Therefore, technical support must be adequate to allow you to be involved in the project, without having to spend long periods of time learning how to use the technology.
- *Your understanding of the pedagogy and strategy of managing the technology:* Teachers need an understanding of the pedagogical issues associated with integrating a medium into the teaching and learning environment. Therefore, something to consider when deciding which media to use is the extent to which you, and other teachers, will need to develop this understanding and

the extent to which a support structure, such as a teaching and learning department, is available.

- *The financial cost:* You need to think about the extent to which your own money will be used. Other project members may already have the required technology, but you may need to purchase some expensive equipment. Are you willing to do this? Can you afford to be involved?
- *Are you risk adverse or risk seeking?* Before committing to being involved in a flexible learning project, do a personal "costs versus benefits" analysis. Are you willing to take the necessary risks?

Institution-Related Factors

A project team seeking the support of an institution's senior management needs to be aware of at least four factors that influence managers' educational technology preferences.

1. *Being seen as educational technology leaders:* Institutions exist in a competitive marketplace. It is important to be seen, by prospective students and the general community, as an institution that uses the latest technology. Also, governments are more likely to fund projects that use the latest technology. For example, there are more sources of funding to investigate the integration of the Internet into the educational environment than to fund the development of print-based packages.
2. *The mix of research and technology:* Institutions, in particular universities, are constantly balancing research and teaching. Invariably there are times when the focus of senior management is on research. In such times, obtaining support for educational projects, particularly those with large budgets, can be difficult.
3. *The institution's support structure:* The support structures of an institution, both technical and those that focus on the art and science of teaching and learning, influence the media that are used. For example, if an institution has a license for a particular course management system (Chapter 9), persuasive arguments will have to be presented in order to receive funding for a different system.

4. *Maximizing the return on investment:* As discussed in Topic 1.2, an institution should aim to maximize the return on investment in a project. This involves ensuring that developed resources are useful to as many teachers and students as possible. This can mean management encourages the use of particular media that use the existing technology infrastructure.

Course-Related Factors

The content of a course influences the types of learning opportunities provided, including the media that are used. Some courses have an applied nature. Others focus on theoretical perspectives. While many pure science areas, such as chemistry and physics, emphasize interactions with inanimate objects, those of a more social science nature, such as hotel and tourism management, focus on developing students' abilities to interact with their fellow employees and customers.

Consider a strategic human resource management course designed to develop students' teamwork skills. Such a course can include role-playing scenarios that involve students interacting

- in a face-to-face environment during an on-campus tutorial;
- in a computer-mediated contact environment, such as a Web forum; or
- in a combination of the two environments.

What is important is that media are used that facilitate the development of teamwork skills.

In other courses, interaction among students is not so important and consequently different types of learning opportunities and media can be used. For example, consider a financial management course in which students create profit and loss statements for an investment center, such as a hotel, on the basis of analyzing the financial statements from each of the hotel's profit and cost centers. A variety of media can be used in activities designed to help students create the profit and loss statements:

1. An incomplete profit and loss statement for the investment center and the supporting schedules could be provided on paper. The teacher will assess students' attempts.

2. The entire activity could be completed online, as part of a Web page, and be designed so that students' attempts are instantaneously assessed by the Web site and feedback is given.
3. A combination of paper and a Web site can be used. The supporting schedules are on paper to help students refer to them while completing the Web page profit and loss statement, which is instantaneously assessed by the Web site with feedback.

If the teacher's objective is to assess the students, then an activity of the first type would be appropriate. If the objective is to encourage students to self-evaluate their understandings, then an activity of the third type would be appropriate. Although the second type of activity is possible, it does not take into account the need for students to constantly refer to many schedules while constructing an overall profit and loss statement. This type of activity ignores the difficulties of manipulating multiple schedules on a computer screen.

TOPIC 5.5: USING MEDIA INSTEAD OF A MEDIUM

This topic starts with a description of a real case of using media, rather than one medium, to provide learning opportunities (Exhibit 5.2). My involvement in this project, which was not part of the HTM Project, was as an educational designer.

I advocate the creation of environments where a variety of media are used in the provision of learning opportunities (Exhibit 5.3). The reasons, consistent with a constructivist model of knowledge (Topic 4.2), are as follows:

1. Learning is complex and not the result of encountering only one source of information.
2. The complexity and uniqueness of the learning process for each student mean that students react in different ways to different media at different stages of the development of their understandings.
3. As discussed in Topic 5.3, access to technology and the ability to use it effectively vary among students. By using a variety of media, there is a greater likelihood that each student will be able to select learning opportunities that use technology the student can access and knows how to use.
4. Using a variety of media increases the probability that students other than the main target group can use some of the materials as supplementary resources, therefore helping in maximizing the return on investment (Topic 1.2).

In this handbook, terms such as *print-based learning, online learning,* and *e-learning* are not used. This is because I believe that these terms imply that we can attribute learning to using one particular medium. For example, consider an environment where the core resources are provided using the Internet. This may be called an e-learning environment. The difficulty I have with this and other medium-specific categorizations of learning is that when students successfully pass the course, there is a tendency to conclude that the e-learning environment was the cause. But how can you determine the extent to which the core resources—provided using the Internet—

EXHIBIT 5.2. Integrating Media

The aim was to develop a short course to help professional people employed by national and international companies develop skills associated with being interviewed by journalists. The final package used the following media:

- The Internet to provide notes and activities.
- A paper workbook to provide activities best completed using pen and paper. Also, course notes that it was considered students would find useful in their daily professional lives were included. This eliminated the need to print out Web pages.
- A telephone system that involved students dialing different numbers to role-play scenarios that simulated different types of telephone interviews.
- The teacher—each student was allocated a set number of hours in which they could either phone the teacher to discuss the course, meet face-to-face, or both.

The original intention was to use only the Internet, that is, to use only the latest technology. However, the more we considered the needs, wants, and the technology access of the target audience, the more it became obvious that a variety of well-integrated media was superior to using one medium.

contributed to students' understanding of the course concepts? Maybe the interactions were detrimental to some students and they had to use other resources—such as the teacher, their fellow students, and textbooks—to clarify their thinking. Maybe some students found the Internet-based resources useful only because they had well-developed prior knowledge of the concepts, based on a whole range of different learning opportunities.

Learning is complex and not the result of encountering one source of information. Each person develops an understanding on the basis of prior knowledge and the processes of assimilation and accommodation (Topic 4.2). There is no magic medium that will help all students. Therefore, as educationalists we should embrace variety and maximize the range of media we use to help students learn.

EXHIBIT 5.3. Media Variety

In each of the ten HTM Project courses a variety of media was used. This was because of the consensus among the project team members, and other stakeholders, that each medium offered attributes that when combined with other media created an environment that best met the needs and wants of the students, the teachers, and the institution.

The following media were used in each course:

- Print-based notes for the core learning resource
- Face-to-face meetings on-campus with fellow students and the teacher, which students chose whether to attend
- Face-to-face meetings between the teacher and a student, in the teacher's office, if the student requested a meeting
- Telephone communication between the teacher and students
- E-mail communication between the teacher and students

In addition, three of the courses included a compulsory textbook and a range of media, such as that found in libraries, to use when completing assignments. As the school developed a Web site for each course, using a course management system, it was added to the media used.

KEY POINTS

1. Teachers are crucial to quality learning experiences. Project team members need to remind themselves of this fact.
2. The perception that students are computer and Internet literate, and therefore able to use any computer-based or Internet-based resource, is not always true. Base your decisions about the media you use on an understanding of the capabilities of the students you are developing a resource for.
3. The objective is to help students by using the most effective combination of media.

Chapter 6

Developing Print Resources

Producing print-based, flexible learning resources involves using lecture and tutorial notes as the foundations for package creation. The design specification, which is applied to course content, is based on meeting the educational needs and wants of students. Project success is dependent on the ability of team members to adapt to changing circumstances. For although a nine-stage production process is followed, including the application of a design specification, resource development is chaotic.

OBJECTIVES

1. To explain that a collection of notes that a teacher uses in lectures and tutorials is not equivalent to a flexible learning package but rather is a useful starting point for resource development
2. To describe the advantages and disadvantages, for students, teachers, and institutions, of using and developing print resources
3. To list and explain the key considerations in a nine-stage production process that involves the application of a design to quality content, resulting in a print-learning resource
4. To discuss how a design specification for a print resource focuses on helping students answer these questions:

   - Why am I using this resource?
   - Where am I?
   - Where can I go?
   - What have I seen?

- How does this relate to my world?
- How can I determine if I understand?
- What do other people think?

5. To list questions and issues associated with the maintenance and revision of print resources.

TOPIC 6.1: INTRODUCTION

*A **print resource** is a medium of information distribution that uses the technologies of print and paper.*

This chapter is addressed to teachers, content writers, educational designers, and project managers. Topic 6.2 will be of interest to those thinking about developing print resources, as it discusses the advantages and disadvantages from three perspectives—students, teachers, and institutions. Topics 6.3, 6.4, and 6.5 each focus on an aspect of the development model for flexible learning resources, introduced in Topic 1.4. The design, production, maintenance, and revision processes are discussed.

Print resources vary in size and complexity, with many forming part of a collection of learning opportunities provided using a range of media. The packages developed during the HTM Project (Topic 1.3) are examples of large resources, between 400 and 500 pages, designed to be used as core learning resources. Textbooks, newspapers, and lecture handouts are also examples of print-based resources.

Lecture Notes Are Different from Flexible Learning Notes

Sometimes when teachers are asked to be content writers, they say that they already have the flexible learning notes. Usually they are referring to the teachers' notes and those given to students during on-campus lectures and tutorials. However, in most cases these are not flexible learning notes. Instead, they are a starting point for resource development.

Some reasons why lecture and tutorial notes are not equivalent to flexible learning notes are as follows.

- In general, lecture notes summarize what a teacher says. The notes are designed to be used in conjunction with listening to lectures.
- Flexible learning resources, especially if they are core resources, are designed to support student choice in whether to attend on-campus classes. This has implications for the design of flexible learning notes, compared to on-campus lecture and tutorial notes:
  a. The notes are more comprehensive.
  b. The descriptions of course concepts are integrated with activities designed to encourage self-evaluation of understanding.
  c. There is a greater need to explicitly encourage students to communicate with their peers and the teacher.
- In many countries, copyright regulations for materials distributed in flexible learning resources are more restrictive than those applying to on-campus situations. Material distributed in on-campus lectures and tutorials in accordance with fair use guidelines often cannot be included in a flexible learning package, unless the copyright holders grant explicit permission (see Exhibit 6.1).

EXHIBIT 6.1. Using Existing Resources

Objective 1 of the HTM Project, described in Topic 1.3, was to provide students with a learning environment in which they decided when to attend on-campus classes. This involved the development of core learning resources for ten courses.

The year before the HTM Project, the school created lecture packages. The goal for each course was to collect the teacher's preparation notes and handouts distributed in on-campus lectures and tutorials. At this time, the program of study involved compulsory attendance at weekly lectures and tutorials. The notes were collated to bring a sense of structure to the resources and to help teachers who had not previously taught the courses. There was minimal development of new resources.

The extent to which the lecture packages were used as starting points for the flexible learning packages varied from course to course:

- If the person assigned to be a flexible learning content writer had written most of the lecture pack, it was more likely that it was used in the initial stages of resource development.
- With some courses, changes were made to the syllabi which meant that sections of the lecture packs were no longer relevant.
- Sections of some lecture packs contained material that, while legal to use in on-campus classes, was illegal to include in flexible learning packages. Therefore, although the material could help the content writers, it could not be included in the flexible learning resources without reproduction permissions being obtained.

As an educational designer, I found the lecture packs to be a blessing and a curse. They were a blessing as they gave us a starting point. They were a curse in that some writers wanted to use the materials without a lot of modification. However, on-campus lecture and tutorial notes are not the same as flexible learning notes. This meant that it sometimes took longer to reach agreement with a content writer about the design of a flexible learning package.

Despite the challenges that lecture packages can present to an educational designer, I recommend that they are used as starting points for flexible learning resources. It is better to start with something, rather than just a pen and empty sheets of paper.

TOPIC 6.2: ADVANTAGES AND DISADVANTAGES OF PRINT LEARNING RESOURCES

In this topic, the advantages and disadvantages, for students, teachers, and institutions, of using and developing print learning resources are considered.

Using Print Resources

Characteristics that make print resources attractive to students and teachers include the following:

- Their portability (They are self-contained and relatively strong.)
- Their convenience of use and familiarity (If a person can read, he or she can use the resource.)
- Their relative inexpensiveness, compared to resources such as CD-ROMS that require computer hardware
- The ability to write notes on the pages and highlight sections
- The fact that they are physical items that are visible and can be held
- The ease with which copies can be made
- The fact that a wide selection of print resources exists for most courses (For example, a teacher deciding which textbook to recommend for an events management course can consider the pros and cons of a range of textbooks.)

For students and teachers, the disadvantages of using print resources include

- the large size and weight of resources such as textbooks and course packages; and
- the static nature of print on paper.

The static nature of print means that explaining and understanding certain types of content can be difficult and motivation can be hard to maintain. For example, while a long textual and diagrammatic explanation of group training exercises can be written, ideally students should also participate in such exercises.

A focus on encouraging teachers to use print resources allows an institutional emphasis on providing training and support about educational issues, instead of the technical issues commonly emphasized with computer-based resources. Another institutional advantage is that no technical maintenance is required once the print resources are distributed to students. Compare that, for example, to an Internet-based course management system (Chapter 9) that requires technical maintenance throughout the semester. However, there are disadvantages for an institution in focusing on using print resources. For example, postage costs can be high. A focus on print resources, rather than those based on the latest technology, can result in an institution being perceived by prospective students and government funding bodies as lacking entrepreneurial and innovative spirit.

Developing Print Resources

For students there are advantages in using print resources that were developed by staff of the educational institution they are enrolled in.

- Although learning is a personal struggle, it helps students to know their teachers' interpretations of course concepts.
- The notes, compared to resources developed outside of the institution, are more likely to target content areas students have difficulty understanding. This is because the teachers have the best awareness of the needs and wants of the students. Also, the teachers understand the overall program of study, including the syllabus of each course.
- Compared to resources developed in other countries, the notes are more likely to include examples showing how course concepts relate to students' everyday lives.

The following are some of the advantages for teachers of being involved as content writers in the development of print resources.

- By developing resources, teachers have more opportunity, compared to using purchased resources, to cater to the needs and wants of students (Topic 5.3).
- Through the writing process, teachers further develop their understandings of the course and students' difficulties. Often we

only truly understand something when we need to help others learn.
- Compared to developing computer-based resources, no advanced technical skills are necessary. All that is needed is a pen, paper, and the ability to use word-processing software.

A focus on developing print resources can be advantageous for an institution. Compared to resources based upon more recent technology, the fundamentals of the process are established. Therefore, delays in development timetables are less likely and budgeting can be more precise. However, such a focus can be inconsistent with the desire of institutions to be seen as using the latest educational technology. Also, large-scale print resource development requires a significant and expensive infrastructure to facilitate printing, packaging, and storage.

The Financial Costs of Developing Print Resources

The financial costs of developing a print resource depend on many factors, including

- context-dependent items, such as the salaries of team members and printing costs;
- the extent to which existing institutional capabilities are used, such as a teaching and learning center to provide educational design expertise; and
- the resource scope. For example, the costs of developing a package for an entire course are higher than those for developing notes that target only a few learning objectives.

The following list of the types of financial costs is based on developing a core learning resource for an entire course. Some of the items will not apply when developing smaller resources.

- *Salaries of project team members*
- *Consultancy fees and financial rewards:* Like the salaries of people employed by the institution, the fees that consultants charge, such as those for a stakeholder meeting facilitator (Topic

3.4), can be large. Any financial rewards to content writers also need to be accounted for.

- *Computer hardware and software costs:* These costs are not usually large as people already have the computers and software required.
- *Incidental development costs:* This includes items such as paper and print cartridges. The idea of developing resources on computer and only printing a final copy is a myth. People print out drafts in order to be able to work on them while away from a computer and to see the overall layout. It is easier to spread out pages on a desk than it is to buy enough computer monitors to achieve the same perspective.
- *Duplication costs:* These are costs associated with printing and packaging the resource. They include costs for the paper, the files in which the resources are placed, and printing on the file cover, such as the course name and institution logo.
- *Storage costs:* In some institutions, space is in such short supply that it is necessary to pay for the materials to be stored before distribution to students.
- *Distribution costs:* If the resources are mailed to students, the costs can be large.
- *Copyright fees:* Fees for the reproduction of copyrighted material need to be budgeted for. Such fees can be due each semester the resource is used (Topic 4.6).

TOPIC 6.3: PRODUCTION

In the development model, explained in Topic 1.4, production is the application of a design to quality content. This results in a resource. The focus of this topic is the process of producing print-learning resources. It is assumed that you have identified the part of a course for which a resource will be developed and decided that it will be a print resource.

The complexity of the production process depends on the amount of a course syllabus for which a resource is being developed. Although the examples used in this topic come from the HTM Project, where packages were developed for entire courses, my goal is to describe the process in a general way, therefore helping you identify those stages applicable to your situation. In the following discussion, the term *unit* is used to denote a section of a learning resource.

A **unit** *is a section of a learning resource. It contains topics. The number of units depends on factors such as the number of central themes in a syllabus and the structure of the semester.*

Important things to think about as you start to produce a print resource include the following.

- The project manager drives the production process.
- A development timetable that all project team members commit to is crucial to project success.
- Spend time on creating a dynamic and friendly team environment. Regular lunches away from the institution are not a waste of time. They are opportunities to maintain an effective team.
- Send away applications for permission to reproduce copyrighted items early in the production process.
- Writing the first draft of a unit is challenging. The content writer must receive clear guidance from the educational designer and the support of peer reviewers.
- Well-developed flexible learning notes deserve quality packaging, a professional duplication process, and a commitment to regular maintenance and revision.
- A flexible learning package is a work in progress. Although team members may never be totally satisfied with the package, a time comes when it needs to be completed. It needs to be finalized. When this occurs, ideas for improvements are recorded and considered when the package is revised.

The nine stages of the print resource production process are summarized in Figure 6.1. The following discussions consider each stage in more detail.

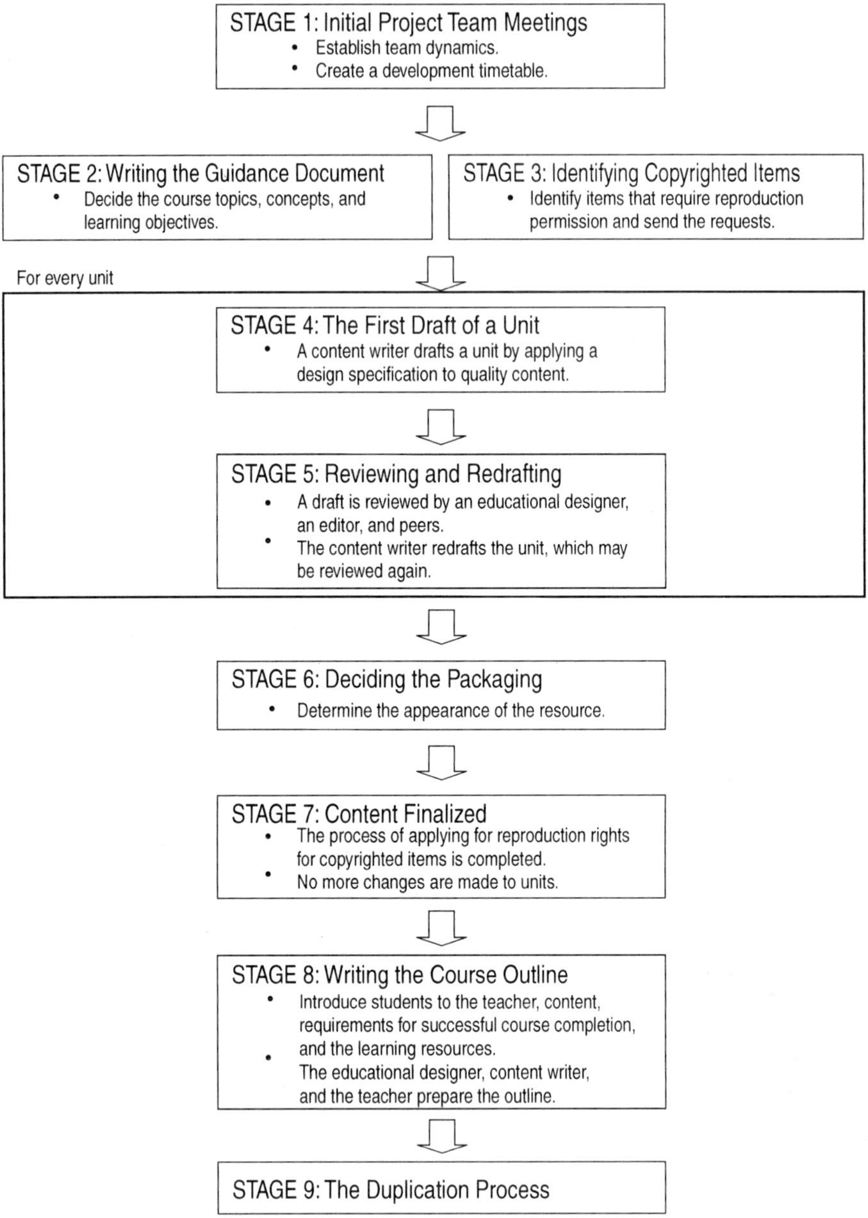

STAGE 1: Initial Project Team Meetings
- Establish team dynamics.
- Create a development timetable.

STAGE 2: Writing the Guidance Document
- Decide the course topics, concepts, and learning objectives.

STAGE 3: Identifying Copyrighted Items
- Identify items that require reproduction permission and send the requests.

For every unit

STAGE 4: The First Draft of a Unit
- A content writer drafts a unit by applying a design specification to quality content.

STAGE 5: Reviewing and Redrafting
- A draft is reviewed by an educational designer, an editor, and peers.
- The content writer redrafts the unit, which may be reviewed again.

STAGE 6: Deciding the Packaging
- Determine the appearance of the resource.

STAGE 7: Content Finalized
- The process of applying for reproduction rights for copyrighted items is completed.
- No more changes are made to units.

STAGE 8: Writing the Course Outline
- Introduce students to the teacher, content, requirements for successful course completion, and the learning resources.
- The educational designer, content writer, and the teacher prepare the outline.

STAGE 9: The Duplication Process

FIGURE 6.1. The Nine Stages of the Print Resource Production Process

Stage 1: Initial Project Team Meetings

The objectives of the first few meetings of the project team are to

- introduce team members to one another;
- make people aware of their roles and those of their colleagues;
- outline the production and design processes; and
- establish a development timetable.

The project manager controls the meetings. Chapter 2 contains information useful to a manager in the initial stages of a project and Topic 3.3 describes people's roles.

The Development Timetable

A development timetable is based upon an awareness of

- the complexity of the planned package;
- the date on which the resource will be distributed to students; and
- the commitments of the project team members, including issues such as people being away from the institution and the teaching loads of content writers.

The following are recommendations about creating a development timetable for a print resource:

- Work back from the date on which students will receive the package.
- A guidance document lists the topics, concepts, and learning objectives for a learning resource (Topic 4.3). It is the document upon which a resource is based. Therefore, ensure that sufficient time is allocated to its creation.
- As more units are developed, the content writers become more familiar with the process. Therefore, the time allocated to each unit is decreased.
- Apply a development model in which more than one unit is developed simultaneously. Although completing the development of one unit before starting another is attractive, in reality there is often not enough time for this to occur.

- A course outline is a document that introduces students to the teacher, the content, the requirements for successful course completion and the learning resources (Topic 4.5). This document is the final part of the resource to be developed.
- Allocate a number of weeks to the duplication and packaging processes.
- Allow for a number of reserve weeks in case of unexpected events.

Table 6.1 is a development timetable for a package developed by one content writer, who also had teaching duties, working with an educational designer and a project manager. It illustrates the application of the recommendations previously discussed to the development of a package for an entire course, like that in the HTM Project (see Exhibit 6.2). The actual dates that would appear in a timetable are replaced in Table 6.1 with references to weeks.

TABLE 6.1. Timetable for the Development of a Print Package

Week	Unit	Activity	End Point
33 to 30		Develop Guidance Document	
29	1	Draft from Content Writer to Educational Designer	
27	1	Review from Educational Designer to Content Writer	
26	2	Draft from Content Writer to Educational Designer	
25	1	Redraft from Content Writer to Educational Designer	Unit 1 Finished
24	2	Review from Educational Designer to Content Writer	
	3	Draft from Content Writer to Educational Designer	
22	2	Redraft from Content Writer to Educational Designer	Unit 2 Finished
	3	Review from Educational Designer to Content Writer	
	4	Draft from Content Writer to Educational Designer	
20	3	Redraft from Content Writer to Educational Designer	Unit 3 Finished

Week	Unit	Activity	End Point
	4	Review from Educational Designer to Content Writer	
	5	Draft from Content Writer to Educational Designer	
18	4	Redraft from Content Writer to Educational Designer	Unit 4 Finished
	5	Review from Educational Designer to Content Writer	
	6	Draft from Content Writer to Educational Designer	
16	5	Redraft from Content Writer to Educational Designer	Unit 5 Finished
	6	Review from Educational Designer to Content Writer	
	7	Draft from Content Writer to Educational Designer	
15	7	Review from Educational Designer to Content Writer	
14	6	Redraft from Content Writer to Educational Designer	Unit 6 Finished
	8	Draft from Content Writer to Educational Designer	
13	7	Redraft from Content Writer to Educational Designer	Unit 7 Finished
	8	Review from Educational Designer to Content Writer	
	9	Draft from Content Writer to Educational Designer	
12	9	Review from Educational Designer to Content Writer	
	10	Draft from Content Writer to Educational Designer	
11	8	Redraft from Content Writer to Educational Designer	Unit 8 Finished
	10	Review from Educational Designer to Content Writer	
	11	Draft from Content Writer to Educational Designer	
10	9	Redraft from Content Writer to Educational Designer	Unit 9 Finished

TABLE 6.1 *(continued)*

Week	Unit	Activity	End Point
	10	Redraft from Content Writer to Educational Designer	Unit 10 Finished
	11	Review from Educational Designer to Content Writer	
	12	Draft from Content Writer to Educational Designer	
9	11	Redraft from Content Writer to Educational Designer	Unit 11 Finished
	12	Review from Educational Designer to Content Writer	
8	12	Redraft from Content Writer to Educational Designer	Unit 12 Finished
		Course outline document developed	
7 to 5		Emergency reserve	
4 to 1		Duplication and packaging	
0		Package to students	

Stage 2: Writing the Guidance Document

The objectives and process of writing a guidance document, which lists the topics, concepts, and learning objectives for which a resource is being developed, are discussed in Topic 4.3.

Stage 3: Identifying Copyrighted Items

In a print resource, you may want to include text extracts, diagrams, and journal articles for which you need to obtain permission from the copyright holders to reproduce. Topic 4.6 discusses the merits of including such materials and the process of obtaining permission.

In stage 3, all copyrighted items must be identified and the process of obtaining permission started. This is because it can take months for permission to be either granted or denied. The identification process occurs at the same time as development of the guidance document (stage 2). The process involves the following steps:

• The educational designer explains to the content writer how to determine which items need reproduction permission.

- The content writer identifies each item. This involves completing a reproduction request form describing where the item will appear in the resource and details about the copyright holder. A copy of the item is attached to the form.
- The educational designer sends to the copyright holder a request for permission to reproduce the item.

Until permission is granted or denied, the project team works on the assumption that all requests will be granted and that the project manager will agree to the conditions stipulated by the copyright holder.

EXHIBIT 6.2. Development Timetables for Print Resources: Theory versus Reality

In the HTM Project, a development timetable was constructed for each of the ten packages. Each timetable allocated

- four weeks to the writing of the guidance document;
- four weeks to the duplication and packaging processes; and
- three weeks were held in reserve.

The number of weeks allocated to the writing of the units varied among courses, with major influences being the number of content writers and the existing commitments of the project team. For example, as the project manager and lead educational designer, I found it difficult to work on more than two course packages simultaneously.

For the most part, development timetables were approximately met, with units being submitted within a few days of the deadlines. However, there were challenges in meeting some of the timetables. I found that the more content writers we had for a package, and the more time we had to develop it, the greater the tendency for deadlines not to be met. Although it was common for the three reserve weeks to be used, for nine of the ten courses the packages were ready for printing before the four weeks allocated to the process. For one course package, significant alterations to the development timetable had to be made due to personnel issues in the school. This package was distributed to students in two parts, the first six units at the start of semester and the last six during the fourth week of the fourteen-week semester.

My advice to project managers is to expect changes in a development timetable. You make a timetable to provide impetus and direction. As long as you have weeks in reserve, and continually encourage team members to approximately meet deadlines, all will work out.

Stage 4: The First Draft of a Unit

Stages 4 and 5 are completed for each unit of a print resource. Writing the first draft of the first unit is a particularly demanding task. It involves developing quality content (Topic 4.3) and applying the design specification (Topic 6.4) for the first time.

Before the writer starts the draft of the first unit, the educational designer explains the design specification. The following points are emphasized:

- If, as the units are written, it becomes apparent that modifying the specification would improve the resource, then changes to the specification are made after consulting with the rest of the team.
- Writing a draft is a difficult and time-consuming task. However, with practice it becomes easier.
- The writer should aim to draft an entire unit of a resource before asking for comments from the educational designer and peer reviewers. In this way the writer experiences the entire process of applying the design and is better able to recommend changes to the specification.

Stage 5: Reviewing and Redrafting

Once a content writer has drafted the first version of a unit (stage 4), the educational designer and peer reviewers consider it. On the basis of their recommendations, the unit is redrafted. Stage 5 can occur more than once. The educational designer is responsible for coordinating the review process. The following guidelines about the process of reviewing a unit in a print resource are for educational designers:

1. The content writer provides an electronic version of the unit.
2. The educational designer considers the draft:

- If the draft needs a significant amount of work, it could be best that the designer meets with the content writer to discuss issues and request a redraft before peer reviewers see it.
- If the draft needs significant changes to the language, an editor modifies it before peer reviewers see it.

- A project assistant makes changes to the electronic version on the basis of the designer's and editor's annotations.

3. The peer reviewers consider the draft, based upon guidelines provided by the educational designer. The reviewers, as course content experts and teachers, consider the unit. Each reviewer gives the educational designer a written document detailing suggested alterations. The educational designer decides whether the recommended changes are significant enough to justify a meeting of the designer, the reviewers, and the content writer.
4. The educational designer meets with the content writer to discuss the draft, indicating parts that need changing and any suggestions for additional content, on the basis of the designer's, editor's, and peer reviewers' considerations.

This four-step process is repeated until the unit is of the required quality. A caveat: For two reasons the educational designer keeps copies of all drafts. First, an idea removed from an early draft may ultimately be used. Second, the drafts are a record of the work of the project team and can be used to resolve misunderstandings (see Exhibit 6.3).

Who Decides the Drafting Process Is Finished?

Deciding when a unit is finished can be a contentious process. It depends on the personalities and professionalism of the team members. My recommendations, in order of decreasing preference, as to who decides when a unit is finished are as follows:

1. The educational designer and content writer jointly decide.
2. The educational designer decides.
3. The project manager decides. The manager usually intervenes only when the project is behind schedule.

Stage 6: Deciding the Packaging

Packaging *consists of items that make up the physical appearance of a resource.*

EXHIBIT 6.3. Reviewing a Unit—Recollections of an Educational Designer

In the HTM Project, I was involved in the reviewing of units as an educational designer and editor.

I had to remind myself that while we were applying a design specification, it was also important for content writers to express their individuality. A design specification is a guide, not a straitjacket, for a content writer.

While focusing on my primary role as educational designer, I would also suggest content and examples for units. I believe that a designer who shows an interest in the content is more effective than someone who focuses only on educational issues.

The peer review process worked better than I expected. Its effectiveness is dependent on the ability of reviewers to offer constructive critiques and the ability of writers to accept suggestions. The majority of reviewers submitted written reports to me. I would then discuss these with the writer. This desire for providing indirect feedback could be a cultural preference. In other cultures the preference could be for meetings between reviewers and writers.

The project assistant's word processing and diagram creation expertise was a significant benefit. The ability to quickly update a unit allowed the content writers to focus on the writing process.

The majority of the 120 units (12 per package) went through one major redraft. The few units that required two or three major redrafts were typically the first ones that a content writer wrote.

The packaging for a print resource is dependent on its type. For example, it could be a pamphlet or materials for an entire course. Exhibit 6.4 describes the issues considered when deciding the packaging for the HTM Project print packages.

Detailed consideration should be given to packaging. Project teams spend significant time and resources developing quality educational materials, and it is only right that they are presented in professionally created packages.

Stage 7: Content Finalized

Three weeks before the duplication process (stage 9), the project manager stops the process of requesting reproduction rights for copyrighted material (stage 3). Although the requests would have been

EXHIBIT 6.4. The Packaging of a Print Resource— Things to Think About

The packaging for the HTM Project print resources had a high degree of consistency so that we could achieve cost savings by ordering large quantities.

The Type of File

- We had a choice of two- or three-hole files, and decided to use three-hole for greater page stability.
- Each file included an inner sleeve to hold additional materials and an outer spine sleeve for a course description, which consisted of the name of the university, the course title, and the academic year printed on cardboard.

The Printing on the File

- All files had the name of the school and the university logo printed on the cover. Black-and-white printing was used to reduce costs. As all courses had the same file, we achieved a cost reduction by being able to order large quantities.

The Dividers

- Rigid cardboard was used for all fourteen dividers (course outline, twelve units, appendixes) and tabs were cut to help students identify the units.
- The unit number was printed on a divider tab, and on the rest of the divider the unit's learning objectives and keywords were printed. On the divider for the course outline, the teacher's contact details and the suggested study schedule were printed.

The Type of Paper

- Seventy-five grams per square meter (gsm) white paper was used. A lighter, and consequently cheaper, paper was available. However, printing trials showed that to prevent the print from being seen through the page, it was necessary to use a heavier paper.

sent months before, it is likely that no replies will have been received for some. These cases need to be identified, and the educational designer will organize the removal of the items and content modification.

The resources have now reached the final stage. At this point, no changes are made unless a significant error or omission is identified. The master electronic versions of the units are held by the project manager.

Stage 8: Writing the Course Outline

The content writer, the teacher, and the educational designer write the course outline (Topic 4.5). This document introduces students to the teacher, the content, the requirements for successful course completion, and the learning resources.

Stage 9: The Duplication Process

If the print resource is any larger than a few pages and is to be given to more than ten students, you will want to duplicate it using professional printing facilities. The majority of printing centers, including those in institutions, will send you a test print. It is crucial that someone in the project team looks at each page to ensure no misalignments have occurred. Such care is necessary to ensure that the hard work of the team is not spoiled by small, yet noticeable, errors. For example, in the HTM Project, the master electronic version was submitted through an intranet system to the university's print center. Small misalignments occurred that resulted in tables and diagrams splitting across pages. By giving a team member responsibility for proofing the test copy, such imperfections were corrected.

TOPIC 6.4: DESIGN

In the development model, explained in Topic 1.4, a design is applied to quality content to create a resource. The process, described in Topic 6.3, of applying a design is called production. In this topic the focus shifts to thinking about design. A design specification document is the end result of considering design issues.

The complexity of a design is dependent on the amount of a course syllabus for which a resource is being developed. Although the examples used in this topic come from the HTM Project, where packages were developed for entire courses, my goal is to describe issues in a general way, thereby helping you identify those sections applicable to your situation. In the following discussion, the term *unit* is used to denote a section of a learning resource.

The following items and events are important in ensuring a good design specification:

- A design specification can be altered as the skills and experiences of team members develop.
- The medium is print. Therefore, think about how best the characteristics of the medium can be exploited to help students learn.
- Look at print resources that you find attractive. Consider whether some of the designs can be used in the resource you are developing.
- When in doubt, ask some colleagues and students for their opinions. Informal small-scale surveys are a quick way of refining a design.
- A design is a balance between consistency and variety. Consistency is required to help students use a resource. Variety is needed to motivate students and help them understand course content.

The majority of the examples in this topic are from the unit titled "Overview of the Strategic Management Process," which was the third unit of twelve in the package developed for the strategic management course during the HTM Project. Design is a challenging topic to describe and understand. I recommend that you read Topic 4.4 in conjunction with this topic.

Why Am I Using This Resource?

To help students know why they are using a resource, you can place an outline at the start of each unit. This consists of a couple of introductory paragraphs, short descriptions of the topics, and the unit's learning objectives. Guidelines for writing learning objectives are presented in Topic 4.4. As you read the following example of an introductory paragraph, note the inclusive and personal style of the language and how attention is drawn to a difficult topic.

In Unit 3 our main task is to have an introductory look at the strategic management process. We will consider strategic analysis, strategic choice, and strategy implementation as the three interrelated parts of the strategic management process.

We will also examine competitive advantage because for most organizations this is a key issue—creating and sustaining an advantage over the competition is crucial to both financial success and long-term development. Finally we will make a start on a difficult topic—what makes strategic management "effective." (Reproduced with permission from the Strategic Management flexible learning package, The School of Hotel and Tourism Management at The Hong Kong Polytechnic University, Hong Kong.)

Where Am I? Where Can I Go? What Have I Seen?

The following techniques can be used in print resources to help students answer three questions: Where am I? Where can I go? What have I seen?

- A *table of contents* that lists the topics and subtopics
- A *header,* which appears in the top corner of each page, that details the name of the course, the unit number, and the page number
- A *unit outline*
- An *index* that is created by a content writer to ensure that appropriate terms are selected

- *Consistent heading levels and styles,* such as those indicating a topic, a subtopic, or a case study, to help students identify sections and understand the relationships among them
- Throughout a unit, *sentences that remind students* where they are and how the content relates to what they have read and what they are yet to read

In the following example, the first two paragraphs appear at the start of a topic titled "The Strategic Management Process." The third paragraph appears at the end of the topic.

This topic looks at how strategic management can be viewed as an ongoing process that has three parts: strategic analysis, strategic choice, and strategy implementation.

So far in the course we have looked at strategic planning, strategic leadership, and corporate culture. Now we need to move on to examine the main stages in the strategic management process. Our aim is to understand how strategy is planned, managed, and implemented and also to relate the issues to some organizations in hospitality/tourism industries. . . .

Now let's look at each of the three parts of the process in a little more detail and identify the main issues that have to be resolved at different stages of the process. Later in the course we will get more detailed and work through some tools and techniques that are of practical use. (Reproduced with permission from the Strategic Management flexible learning package, The School of Hotel and Tourism Management at The Hong Kong Polytechnic University, Hong Kong.)

The following extract appears at the end of the unit "Overview of the Strategic Management Process" after an objective checklist designed to let students self-evaluate their understandings. Notice the language style.

We are a quarter of the way through the course. At this stage we have covered all the material to allow you to complete the first assignment. If there are some parts of the course which we have covered so far but which you are not happy about, do something now!

I hope you feel confident that you have mastered this unit. Do not expect to get every self-exercise right the first time. Have a go at the self-exercises, check your answers against my responses, and reflect on them. (Reproduced with permission from the Strategic Management flexible learning package, The School of Hotel and Tourism Management at The Hong Kong Polytechnic University, Hong Kong.)

How Does This Relate to My World?

In print resources, two techniques can be used to help students answer this question. These techniques are "something to think about" sections and refer to local businesses throughout the notes. A "something to think about" section has the following characteristics:

- It describes a real example of the application of concepts explained in the unit.
- The description does not have to explicitly relate the example to the concepts. Instead, by its position on the page, directly after the concept explanation, students are encouraged to realize the relationships themselves.
- It finishes with a question to prompt students to self-evaluate their understandings, or to encourage debate among students, or both.

The following "something to think about" section, titled "Genryoko Sushi—Competitive Advantage," appeared at the end of a topic about competitive advantage.

You may well have eaten at a Genryoko Sushi—read about the company and think about what it is that gives them a competitive advantage.

The Global Food Culture Group Limited operates two Japanese restaurant chains in Hong Kong, Genryoko Sushi and Suishaya.

Suishaya restaurants specialize in Japanese specialties such as barbecue, teppanyaki, shabu-shabu, sashimi, and sushi. Genryoku Sushi specializes in selling sushi with customers helping themselves to the food from a revolving belt. The restaurants are located in prime sites in Kowloon, Hong Kong Island, and (to a minor extent) the New Territories.

From a starting point in 1990, by 1998 there were twenty Genryoko Sushi restaurants catering to young professionals and people looking for affordable Japanese food in a stylish but informal environment. Typically the standard menu includes thirty sushi, seven appetizers, and six sashimi dishes with ongoing product development. The concept has proved very successful and there are often long queues at peak times. The restaurant has a strong "club" mentality that is enhanced by loyalty cards, which can be used to accumulate bonus points for various benefits (discounts on food prices and also gifts, invitations to members-only parties, and activities).

The company is not alone in the market for Japanese food—there are many upmarket restaurants, independent restaurants, and three chains that compete directly: Mingen Japanese Sushi Restaurant, Genki Sushi, and Genwa Sushi.

This company has developed over a ten-year period. What competitive advantages will it need for the next ten years? (Reproduced with permission from the Strategic Management flexible learning package, The School of Hotel and Tourism Management at The Hong Kong Polytechnic University, Hong Kong.)

The following "something to think about" section, titled "Implementation at Chek Lap Kok Airport," appeared at the end of a topic about the management of strategic change.

I am sure you remember the controversy that accompanied the opening of the new airport at Chek Lap Kok in July 1998. Read about some of the issues and think about what needed doing to ensure implementation went smoothly.

Before the airport could start operating on July 6, there was intensive planning by the Airport Authority (AA), its contractors, service providers, airlines, commercial tenants, and government departments. This was coordinated by the AA within the framework of an integrated program that aimed to achieve a smooth transition from construction, testing, and commissioning of facilities and systems to full airport operation. Within this program, the Airport Operational Readiness (AOR) Program identified and monitored the progress of activities that were considered essential to the airport opening, such as staff recruitment and training, the development of operational policies and procedures, and airport user charges.

The AOR Program also included five airport trials between January and June. These culminated in a full trial in June that involved 12,000 volunteers, AA staff, thirty-five airlines, new airport business communities, and government departments. The trials aimed to identify problems and ensure a smooth opening.

A mobilization and move plan was developed by the AA to relocate plant, equipment, and personnel from Kai Tak to Chek Lap Kok. The plan was developed in consultation with NAPCO, the Civil Aviation Department, and other key agencies, including the Police, Transport Department, Marine Department, Highways Department, Hong Kong Observatory, and the AA's many business partners. The mobilization and move took sixty days prior to the airport opening and culminated in a night move phase held from 5:30 p.m. on Sunday, July 5, to 6:30 a.m. on Monday, July 6.

Think about how, despite this careful planning, problems relating to both passenger and cargo services occurred when the airport opened. (Reproduced with permission from the Strategic Management flexible learning package, The School of Hotel and Tourism Management at The Hong Kong Polytechnic University, Hong Kong.)

Local businesses can be mentioned when providing examples of the application of concepts. Such descriptions differ from those in "something to think about" sections in two ways. First, the descriptions are not as detailed, and second, the businesses are mentioned within paragraphs, rather than in a separate section. The following extract illustrates how the concept of branding was related to business examples students were familiar with.

> We often associate a strong brand name with a competitive advantage—for example, Rainforest Cafe, Planet Hollywood, Café de Coral, and Maxim's, all actively manage their brand to try to attract and maintain customers. Branding is a widely used competitive method and one that relies on a strong marketing department, a well-defined product, and sustainable service standards. (Reproduced with permission from the Strategic Management flexible learning package, The School of Hotel and Tourism Management at The Hong Kong Polytechnic University, Hong Kong.)

How Can I Determine If I Understand?

The following are techniques to use in print resources to help students answer this question:

- An *objective checklist* at the end of a unit that asks students the question, "Do you believe that you can achieve the objective?" The student selects "yes" or "no" for each objective.
- *Self-exercises* as described in Topic 4.4.
- Include *discussion points* for use in face-to-face tutorials and computer-mediated contact environments (Chapter 8).

What Do Other People Think?

To help students develop their understandings, it is important to provide them with opportunities to

- discuss matters with their fellow students and the teacher;
- hear and read about the experiences of industry-based people; and
- realize that experts have differing views.

The following are techniques to use in print resources to help students determine what other people think:

- *Summarize the work of experts.* A content writer should have a good awareness of recent articles in academic journals and trade publications. The experts' views can be summarized and included in the units, along with the full details of where students can obtain the articles.

- *Integrate a textbook* into a unit by including "read the textbook" sections. These describe the pages to be read and emphasize particularly relevant parts. Such tight integration, compared to only listing textbook sections at the start or end of a unit, will help students relate the textbook to the unit notes.
- *Include discussion points* to activate debate either in face-to-face tutorials or in computer-mediated contact environments (Chapter 8).
- *Refer students to Web sites* where the views of industry-based people are presented. The references must include more than just the Web site address. Each reference also needs to explain why students should visit the site.

General Educational Guidelines

The following are general educational design issues to consider when developing a print resource:

- *Make sure copyrighted material is integrated.* In stage 3 of the production process (Topic 6.3), I describe how the project team assumes that reproduction requests will be granted. Then if permission is not received, the material is removed and alternative content written (stage 7). This assumption is made to avoid the situation of copyrighted material being slotted in only once reproduction permission is received. A slotting-in approach results in a disjointed unit.
- *Use consistent terminology.* In most courses, some concepts have a number of different names that are equally valid. It is important for students to be aware of the different names. However, having stated them, the content writer should from then on use only one of them. For example, "Flexible learning, also called distance learning or distributed learning, involves providing choice to students and teachers. From now on in these course notes, I use the term flexible learning."
- *Simple diagrams help understanding.* Often a simple diagram can help students understand the relationships among concepts and also improve the page design by breaking up what would

otherwise be pages of solid text. For example, understanding the development model, in Topic 1.4, is helped by Figure 1.1. Other examples are the cartoons in this handbook, which are simple drawings used to illustrate concepts in a humorous way and to provide variety in design.

- *Support students who want to go beyond the syllabus.* A unit should be designed to support students who want to develop a greater understanding of a topic than that necessary to pass the course. Some students will want to go deeper purely because they are interested. Others will have chosen a topic for an assignment and therefore be required to develop a richer understanding. In print resources there are a variety of ways of supporting such students, for example, a "further reading" section at the end of a unit that lists sources of more detailed information and "if you are interested" boxes that appear throughout a unit and include details of additional readings.
- *Practice what you preach.* A print resource should be an example of best practice in academic standards. Quite rightly, teachers expect students to use an acceptable referencing style, as well as acknowledging all sources, in their assignments. Such standards also apply to print resources. For example, students who are uncertain of how to reference a particular type of article should be able to refer to the resource for an example.

Style Guidelines for Print Resources

This topic concludes by considering the style of the pages in a print resource, that is, the look and feel of the pages. Ideally a graphic designer is part of a project team. However, the reality is that few projects in educational institutions employ graphic designers who specialize in educational print resources.

The following style guidelines evolved during the HTM Project in which a specialist graphic designer was not employed.

- *Do not use words that imply a page position.* For example, "As you can see above in Figure 2" will be incorrect if Figure 2 is moved to a different page during the pagination procedure that occurs just before printing.
- *Refer to parts of a resource by their titles, rather than page numbers.* For example, instead of "For a more detailed discussion of

service quality, refer to page 16," write, "For a more detailed discussion of service quality, refer to Topic 15.3: The Dimensions of Service Quality." Although using page numbers is more specific, maintaining the accuracy of the page references during maintenance and revision cycles can be difficult. As with many aspects of design, you need to achieve a balance—in this case between providing specific references and ease of maintenance and revision.

- *Use line drawings rather than photos.* A photo that looks good on a computer screen often becomes a mass of indistinguishable shades of gray when printed to standards common in educational institutions.
- *What is not on a page is as important as what is.* White space helps readability. For example, tables can be more readable when fewer lines are used for borders. Also, white space can encourage students to scribble notes. Students should be encouraged, by the teacher and implicitly by the design, to highlight and annotate.
- *Use a variety of techniques to produce a readable page.* A balance needs to be achieved. A page should not be a continuous stream of text. Neither should it include so many styles that it appears disjointed. You are not producing an academic journal article—but neither are you producing lecture overheads. Techniques to use include
  — consistently using three or four heading levels;
  — having one central theme in each paragraph;
  — bullet points;
  — tables;
  — diagrams;
  — indented paragraphs for extracts from book and articles; and
  — shading and boxes to highlight definitions and important concepts.
- *Minimize the use of bold and italics, and do not use all capital letters.* Such techniques have a role in distinguishing the heading levels in a document, and bold and italics are useful ways of emphasizing words. However, the more they are used, the less effective they are.

TOPIC 6.5: MAINTENANCE AND REVISION

In Topic 1.4, maintenance is defined as making small changes to any combination of the quality content (Topic 4.3), the design (Topic 6.4), and the production process (Topic 6.3). It usually relates to time-dependent matters, such as semester dates. On the other hand, revision involves making larger changes. It is usually an outcome of evaluating the use of a resource. For example, after a resource has been used, the teacher may decide that the learning objectives of a unit need to be changed to better reflect recent industry events. Such a change would ripple through the unit, resulting in changes to the content and possibly the design specification.

A print resource should undergo a maintenance program every time the course is taught. For example, an HTM Project course ran once every academic year. Each time it was necessary to ensure that the print resource, particularly the course outline (Topic 4.5), was up to date.

A revision process should occur at least once every two years. A syllabus changes as a result of new research and industry events. This is particularly the case with courses of a social science nature, such as many of those offered in a hotel and tourism management school, where the relationships between the syllabi and the industry are strong.

Although an educational designer or project assistant can complete most maintenance requirements, revision requires a content writer.

Maintenance Issues

The following are questions to ask and issues to consider when planning the maintenance of a print resource:

- Are all reproduction permissions for copyrighted materials still valid? If some are not, an application for an extension needs to be made (maintenance) or the item removed, resulting in a revision process.
- If a textbook is integrated with a print resource, its availability needs to be checked. If a textbook that was used as a core resource is no longer available, a revision process is necessary.
- In addition to any textbook, references to other resources, such as Web sites, need to be checked.

- Dates in the course outline, for example in the suggested study schedule and in the assignment submission section, need to be changed.
- Consider whether assignments in the course outline should be changed. Any changes need to be made by a content writer.
- Spelling and grammatical errors always occur in print resources. Teachers should be asked to annotate their copies. At the end of the semester, the copy can be given to the project assistant to make corrections.
- The more times a resource is maintained, the greater the likelihood that there will be confusion about which is the most up-to-date version. The person with the responsibility for organizing the duplication of resources should also be responsible for distributing to teachers the latest version. All efforts must be made to avoid the all-too-common situation of a teacher using a version older than the one students have.

Revision Issues

The following are questions to ask and issues to consider when planning the revision of a print resource:

- If copyrighted material is removed, a content writer will either need to write replacement content or find a replacement item for which reproduction permission can be obtained.
- When a textbook that is integrated with a print resource is no longer available, a content writer needs to consider the extent to which a new textbook can replace the old, and the extent to which new content needs to be written.
- Changes to the content may be necessary after the teacher and students have used the resource. These changes can be significant. For example, as a result of marking students' examination papers, a teacher concludes that most students did not develop a sufficient understanding of an important concept. In order to help future students, major changes to the notes may be required.
- Content can rapidly become dated and irrelevant in social science areas, such as hotel and tourism. For example, the use of the Internet in the hotel industry continues to rapidly evolve.

Companies discussed in examples and exercises may have gone out of business since the resource was written. This is a key reason why it is important to ensure a revision process occurs at least once every two years.

- All references to material that is removed when a resource is being revised also need to be removed. For example, if Figure 2 is removed because it was a copyrighted diagram and the reproduction rights have expired, all references to Figure 2 have to be removed and the numbering of remaining figures revised. For example, Figure 3 becomes Figure 2.

KEY POINTS

1. Print resources continue to be developed despite the Internet. This is because they offer many advantages for students and teachers that cannot be offered as easily using computer-based technologies.
2. Be systematic when producing a resource because some issues, such as applying for reproduction permissions, take months to complete.
3. First impressions count. Therefore, give careful thought to the packaging of notes.
4. A content writer's role does not end once a print resource is developed. Instead, the role is ongoing through the maintenance and revision processes.

Chapter 7

Developing and Using Web Sites

For students, the World Wide Web is a useful information source. This is particularly the case when teachers act as Web advisors.

An eight-stage production process can be used to create a course Web site. Such a site may have many Web pages, each containing navigation and content elements. The development process is complex, and the project team has to focus on meeting the educational needs and wants of students.

OBJECTIVES

1. To explain the value in integrating Web sites other than course-specific sites into curricula, for which teachers act as Web advisors encouraging effective and efficient use of the World Wide Web
2. To describe the advantages and disadvantages for students, teachers, and institutions of using and developing Web sites
3. To list and explain the key considerations in an eight-stage course Web site production process that involves the application of a design to quality content
4. To discuss how a design specification for a course Web site focuses on helping students learn
5. To list questions and issues associated with the maintenance and revision of course Web sites

TOPIC 7.1: INTRODUCTION

A **Web site** *is an electronic source of information arranged as intercon-
nected Web pages that usually reside on one Web server. A Web site is accessible through the Internet, an intranet, or both.*

*The **Internet** is an electronic network that facilitates the transmission and
exchange of information. The World Wide Web is part of the Internet.*

*An **intranet** is a private electronic network based on protocols similar to
those of the Internet. However, unlike the Internet, access is restricted to au-
thorized people.*

This chapter is particularly relevant for people involved in the development of course Web sites. In Topic 7.2, the advantages and disadvantages of using and developing Web sites are considered from the perspectives of students, teachers, and institutions. Topic 7.3 focuses on
integrating non-course-specific Web sites into curricula. Topics 7.4,
7.5, and 7.6 focus on applying the flexible learning resource development model introduced in Topic 1.4 to course Web sites.

TOPIC 7.2: ADVANTAGES AND DISADVANTAGES
OF WEB SITES

In this topic, the advantages and disadvantages for students, teachers, and institutions of using and developing Web sites are considered.

Using Web Sites

Characteristics of the World Wide Web attractive to students and
teachers include

- the large number of Web sites and the variety of information
  available on them;
- the fact that information retrieval is fast and convenient, compared to alternatives such as visiting a physical library;
- the opportunity to experience a wide diversity of opinions;
- the increasing integration of animations, video, and audio as the
  Internet becomes the medium of media (Levinson, 1999); and
- Web sites that have interactive activities where people change
  variables and instantaneously see the effects.

Using Web sites also presents challenges to students and teachers:

- The large number of Web sites can result in people becoming distracted and lost in a mass of information. Search and analysis strategies are important in using the Web as an effective and efficient resource.
- Access to Internet-enabled computers is only partially determined by students and teachers. The power and telecommunications infrastructure is dependent on government policies.
- No universal standards exist for Web site design. Therefore, it can be difficult for people to know where they are in a Web site, where they can go, and where they have been. Navigation methods on one site may be different than on the next.
- Annotating a Web site and highlighting sections is difficult. Even when appropriate software is used, the process is not as intuitive as writing on paper.
- Compared to many resources, it is expensive to buy an Internet-enabled computer. There are also the ongoing costs of Internet access, such as Internet Service Provider charges and, in some countries, timed phone calls.

Encouraging teachers to use Web sites is consistent with an institution's desire to be seen as using the latest educational technology. However, there are costs. For example, a training and support infrastructure is required to promote effective and efficient use of the Web. Also, an institution needs to regularly upgrade computer hardware and software.

Developing Course Web Sites

For students, there are advantages in using Web sites developed by staff of the educational institution they are enrolled in. These advantages are described in the corresponding section, titled "Developing Print Resources," in Topic 6.2. Using such sites also has challenges. For example, not every course Web site is adequately integrated into the curriculum and maintained. Sometimes a site is used to distribute information that otherwise would be distributed on paper. This is a valid use of a Web site as long as students are aware of the policy before enrolling.

For teachers involved as content writers in developing Web sites, the advantages include more opportunities, compared to using non-course-specific sites, of catering to the needs and wants of students (Topic 5.3), and also further developing their understandings of courses and students' difficulties. For an institution, developing course Web sites can help prospective students to perceive an institution as being actively engaged in using the latest technology to help students. However, the costs of creating and maintaining Web sites are generally greater than those for resources such as print-based packages. As with any evolving field, the development process is less established and therefore more open to unexpected costs and delays.

The Roles of Course Web Sites

A course Web site may contain thousands of Web pages or just one. The value of a site depends on the extent to which it fulfills its roles. It does not depend on the number of Web pages or the extent to which interactive exercises, animations, audio, and video are used. Some of the potential roles of a course Web site are as

- a source of course notes;
- a database of frequently asked questions;
- a computer-mediated contact environment (Chapter 8) where students communicate among themselves and with the teacher; and
- a method of distributing information that previously was distributed on paper (see Exhibit 7.1).

The Financial Costs of Developing Course Web Sites

The financial costs of developing a Web site depend on many factors, including

- context-dependent items, such as the salaries of team members;
- the extent to which existing institutional capabilities are used, such as an information technology center to provide Web designers and programmers; and
- the scope of the site. For example, the costs of developing a core resource containing all course notes are higher than those for a site designed to act solely as a computer-mediated contact environment.

EXHIBIT 7.1. Why Web Sites Were Developed

Objective 2 of the HTM Project, as stated in Topic 1.3, was as follows:

To maximize the return on investment in the HTM Project by developing Internet-based learning resources, derived from the core learning resources developed for use in the Bachelor of Arts (Honors) in Hotel and Catering Management (Part-Time) program, for use as supplementary resources in other programs of study.

This was achieved by developing ten course Web sites based upon the print packages developed for the flexible learning students. These are the print packages referred to in Chapter 6. The aim was to develop the Web sites so that they could be used by a wide variety of teachers and students in the school, including

- teachers with on-campus courses similar to those in the flexible learning program of study;
- students enrolled in on-campus courses similar to the flexible learning courses; and
- undergraduate and postgraduate students who wanted to refresh their understandings of particular concepts they had previously learned about.

The following list relates to developing and maintaining a core learning resource for an entire course (if a smaller site is being developed, some of the items will not apply):

- *Salaries of project team members:* Wages are usually the largest cost item. Developing a Web site can involve many people. ranging from those also required for print-based resources, such as content writers and educational designers, to Web designers and programmers.
- *Consultancy fees and any financial rewards for content writers.*
- *Computer hardware and software costs:* Developing a Web site and making it accessible to students has costs. For example, the capturing, editing, and digitizing of audio and video files requires specialized equipment. The delivery of such files requires high-capacity Web servers.
- *Copyright fees,* as discussed in Topic 4.6.
- *Maintenance costs:* For example, a systems engineer maintains the integrity of Web servers.

TOPIC 7.3: USING THE WORLD WIDE WEB

The World Wide Web contains thousands of Web sites that can be used in courses. There are three main reasons why it is important for students to experience Web sites other than course-specific sites developed by their teachers (Williams and McKercher, 1999):

1. As a source of information to help them understand course concepts and, in particular, the application of concepts in the real world
2. To assist in the development of students' general Internet skills, such as how to use Web browsers and evaluate information
3. So that they have an awareness of the applications of the Internet to the industry they are learning about

Many types of Web sites can help students understand course content, such as the sites of businesses, industry associations, government departments, textbook publishers, newspapers, magazines, journals, and electronic libraries.

Teachers acting as Web advisors should direct students to useful sites as well as help and encourage them to develop effective and efficient strategies for using the Web. The following are some useful guidelines for teachers:

- *Explain why a Web site should be visited.* To encourage students to visit a site, provide an explanation that relates the site to course concepts and draws attention to particularly relevant pages.
- *Place references to Web sites throughout course notes.*
- *State the address.* When recommending a Web site, either in an e-mail or on your course Web site, provide an automatic link that students can select and their Web browsers automatically open and the written address, for example, <www.bbc.co.uk>. This is for students who prefer to print out notes and visit Web sites at a later time.
- *Be flexible. Be reactive.* The accessibility and immediacy of the Web supports the use of news-based Web sites to relate daily events to course concepts.

- *Beware of link rot.* Before distributing a learning resource, check that all Web site addresses work. Link rot is particularly common in flexible learning resources that are not maintained.

TOPIC 7.4: PRODUCTION

In the development model explained in Topic 1.4, production is the application of a design to quality content. This results in a resource. The focus of this topic is the process of producing course Web sites. It is assumed that you have identified the part of a course for which a resource will be developed and decided that it will be a Web site.

The complexity of the production process depends on the amount of a course syllabus for which a resource is being developed. Although the examples used in this topic come from the HTM Project, where Web sites for use as supplementary resources were developed for entire courses, the aim is to describe the process in a general way, therefore helping you identify those stages applicable to your situation (Exhibit 7.2).

In Topics 7.4, 7.5, and 7.6 the term *element* is used to denote a part of a Web page. For more discussion about elements, refer to the section The Elements of a Web Site in Topic 7.5.

An **element** is a part of a Web page.

Navigation elements *provide the infrastructure to help answer these questions: Where am I? Where can I go? What have I seen?*

Content elements *are the building blocks for course content. They help answer these questions: Why am I using this resource? How does this relate to my world? How can I determine if I understand? What do other people think?*

As you start to produce a Web site, keep in mind the following issues:

- The project manager controls the production process.
- A development timetable that all team members commit to is crucial for project success.

- Apply for permission to reproduce copyrighted items early in the production process. However, if there is programming code for which reproduction permission needs to be obtained, it must be granted before production starts.
- When evaluating a prototype Web site, watch people using it. This often increases the validity of findings compared to only asking people to describe what they did.
- Test the Web site on as many different configurations of computer hardware and software as possible.
- To maximize the usefulness of a course Web site, have an advertising plan to ensure students know about the site, how it will be used by the teacher, and how it can help them successfully complete the course.

The eight stages of the course Web site production process are summarized in Figure 7.1. The following discussions consider each stage in more detail.

EXHIBIT 7.2. Characteristics of the Web Sites

The Web sites developed in the HTM Project provide many of the examples used in Topics 7.4 and 7.5. The following is a summary of their development:

- A Web site was developed for each of ten courses.
- Each site was developed for delivery on the Internet, the school's intranet, and a CD-ROM.
- Each site contained between 150 and 200 Web pages.
- All sites were developed in the fourth year of the HTM Project.
- Two people completed most of the development work. My roles were project manager, educational designer, and Web designer. Another person was an educational designer and Web designer.
- There was no formal involvement of content writers, as the same content was used as that already developed for the print-based packages.
- Self-exercises were modified to make use of the capabilities of the Internet.
- The sites were not integrated with any computer-mediated contact tools, such as a Web forum or Listserv (Chapter 8).
- The sites were not integrated with a course management system (Chapter 9). However, they were designed to facilitate any future integration.

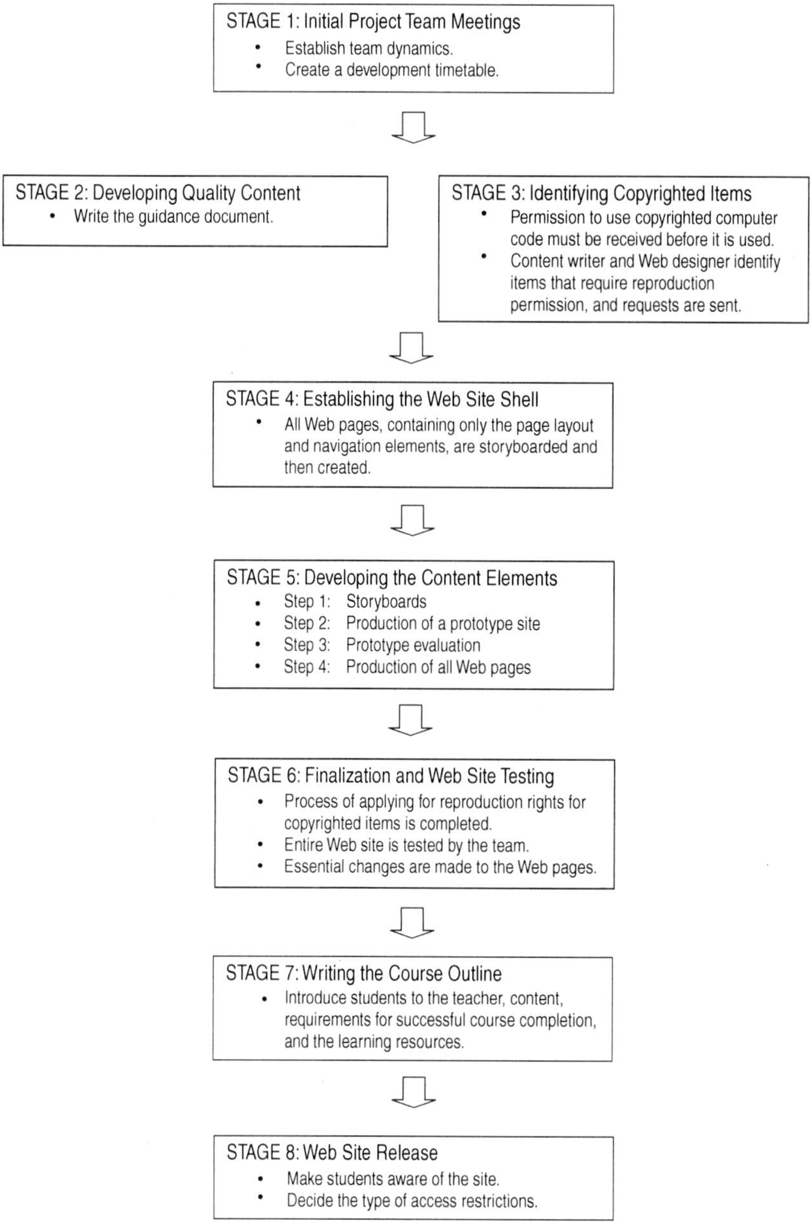

STAGE 1: Initial Project Team Meetings
- Establish team dynamics.
- Create a development timetable.

STAGE 2: Developing Quality Content
- Write the guidance document.

STAGE 3: Identifying Copyrighted Items
- Permission to use copyrighted computer code must be received before it is used.
- Content writer and Web designer identify items that require reproduction permission, and requests are sent.

STAGE 4: Establishing the Web Site Shell
- All Web pages, containing only the page layout and navigation elements, are storyboarded and then created.

STAGE 5: Developing the Content Elements
- Step 1: Storyboards
- Step 2: Production of a prototype site
- Step 3: Prototype evaluation
- Step 4: Production of all Web pages

STAGE 6: Finalization and Web Site Testing
- Process of applying for reproduction rights for copyrighted items is completed.
- Entire Web site is tested by the team.
- Essential changes are made to the Web pages.

STAGE 7: Writing the Course Outline
- Introduce students to the teacher, content, requirements for successful course completion, and the learning resources.

STAGE 8: Web Site Release
- Make students aware of the site.
- Decide the type of access restrictions.

FIGURE 7.1. The Eight Stages of the Course Web Site Production Process

Stage 1: Initial Project Team Meetings

The objectives of the first few meetings of the project team are to

- introduce team members to one another;
- make people aware of their roles and those of their colleagues;
- outline the production and design processes; and
- establish a development timetable.

I have been involved in projects in which the whole team never met. Instead the manager would meet with the content writer and educational designer and have separate meetings with the Web designer and Web programmer. I do not recommend such an approach. Teams are most effective when all members meet and feel able to approach one another throughout the project.

The project manager controls the meetings. Chapter 2 contains information useful to a manager in the initial stages of a project and Topic 3.3 describes people's roles.

The Development Timetable

The purpose of the timetable is to make team members aware of significant targets such as when 25 percent, 50 percent, 75 percent, and 100 percent of Web pages should be completed. In stage 5, the project manager creates another timetable that focuses on the steps involved in creating the content elements for each Web page.

The following are recommendations for creating a development timetable:

- Work back from the date on which students will start to access the site.
- A guidance document lists the topics, concepts, and learning objectives for a learning resource (Topic 4.3). It is the document upon which a Web site is based. Therefore, ensure that sufficient time is allocated to its creation.
- The quality of the Web site shell, which includes the navigation elements, is a key determinant of site usability. Therefore, significant time should be allocated to its design and production (stage 4).

- Apply a development model in which Web pages are produced simultaneously. As the team becomes familiar with the production process, the rate of page completion increases.
- A course outline is a document that introduces students to the teacher, the content, the requirements for successful course completion, and the learning resources (Topic 4.5). This document is the final part of the course resources developed.
- Allocate a number of weeks to test the site (stage 6).
- Allow a number of reserve weeks in case of unexpected events.

Stage 2: Developing Quality Content

Quality content is information that is accurate and relates to the sections of the course syllabus for which a Web site is being developed. Such content may already exist due to the production of a print resource (Chapter 6). Otherwise, a guidance document needs to be written. The objectives and process of writing this document, which lists the topics, concepts, and learning objectives for which a resource is being developed, are discussed in Topic 4.3.

Stage 3: Identifying Copyrighted Items

Copyright and Web site development is an evolving field with many uncertainties and differences in law among countries. You need to discuss matters with experts in your institution.

When developing a Web site, content writers and Web designers may want to include text extracts, diagrams, photos, audio clips, and video clips for which reproduction permission needs to be obtained. The process of requesting reproduction rights is similar to that outlined for print resources in Topic 6.3. A discussion of the merits and process of including such materials appears in Topic 4.6.

Web sites have the added issue, compared to print resource development, of the use of copyrighted programming code. For example, the computer code for a particular type of activity may be copyrighted. Web designers and programmers need to be aware of when they are writing raw code, that is, code written using open computer languages and standards, and when they are using or adapting copyrighted code. It is crucial that permission to use copyrighted code is granted before it is used. Code must not be used on the assumption that permission will be granted, as having to change code later in the project can significantly affect the development schedule.

Stage 4: Establishing the Web Site Shell

A Web site shell contains all Web pages planned for a site. Each page is empty except for

- elements that are in all pages, such as tables and frames used to define the page layout; and
- the navigation elements that provide the infrastructure to help answer these questions: Where am I? Where can I go? What have I seen?

The shell structure is based on the design specification (Topic 7.5) (see Exhibit 7.3 and Figure 7.2).

By producing the Web site shell, a project team is able to test the proposed navigational structure. A good structure is a key criterion for a useful Web site. The following steps are involved in developing a shell:

- Before any computer-based development, the Web pages are storyboarded. This involves sketching each page on a separate piece of paper so that they can be arranged, linked, and altered by team members (Figure 7.3).
- The shell is produced by the Web designer and placed on a Web server. Project team members evaluate the structure and changes are made.

Stage 5: Developing the Content Elements

Stage 5 is the longest of the eight stages in the production process. It involves the development of the content elements for all Web pages and their placement in the Web site shell.

Step 1: Storyboards

Before any computer-based development, storyboards are completed. This involves adding sketches of the content elements to the storyboards developed in stage 4. These do not show the actual con-

EXHIBIT 7.3. A Web Site Shell

Figure 7.2 illustrates the shell for one Web page developed for the strategic management site in the HTM Project. The same page layout was used for all Web pages. As shown in Figure 7.2, the layout consisted of a number of tables within tables, designed for a screen resolution of 800 pixels by 600 pixels or higher. The following are the navigational elements of the Web pages:

- The buttons "The Homepage Strategic Management," "Index," and "FAQ" (Frequently-Asked Questions) on all Web pages
- A "Top" button at the end of each page that when selected returned the student to the top of the page
- A header statement, in this case "Subtopic 6.1.3: Suppliers"
- A topic button, in this case "Topic 6.1: The Operating Environment"
- A number of subtopic buttons, in this case four
- A dot graphic indicating the current section on the computer screen
- For each topic and subtopic button, an underlined v that was blue if the section had not been visited and red if it had been visited

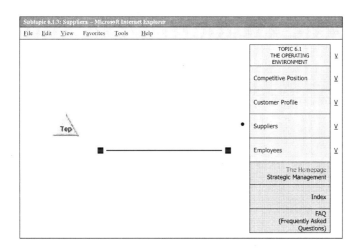

FIGURE 7.2. A Web Page from the Shell for the Strategic Management Web Site, Developed in the HTM Project (*Source:* Reproduced with permission from the Strategic Management flexible learning package, The School of Hotel and Tourism Management at The Hong Kong Polytechnic University, Hong Kong.)

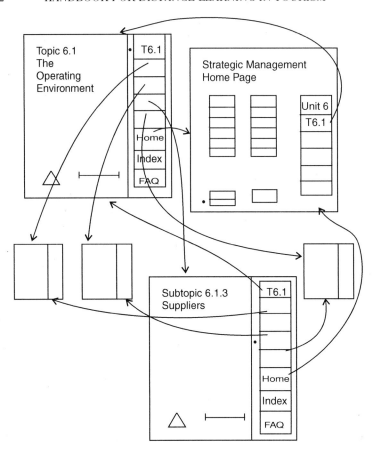

FIGURE 7.3. Storyboards for the Web Site Shell in the Strategic Management Web Site, in the HTM Project

tent. Rather, they show the relative positions of the elements (Figure 7.4). Team members review the storyboards.

Step 2: Production of a Prototype Site

A prototype site contains sufficient Web pages to provide a close-to-real experience for those involved in evaluating it. For each page, the following occurs:

- The content elements are produced by applying the design specification (Topic 7.5) to quality content (stage 2).
- The content writer, educational designer, and Web designer review each page.

Step 3: Prototype Evaluation

The educational designer coordinates the evaluation of the prototype site by a small group of students. The results of the evaluation

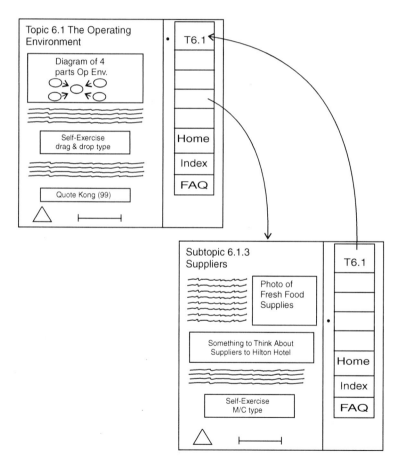

FIGURE 7.4. Storyboards of Web Pages Illustrating the Relative Positions of Content Elements for the Strategic Management Web Site, in the HTM Project

may lead to changes to the design specification and consequently the design of the Web site shell (stage 4), the design of content elements (stage 5), or both.

Step 4: Production of All Web Pages

The Web pages in the prototype are modified on the basis of the evaluation findings. All remaining Web pages are then developed.

The Project Manager's Roles

The project manager tracks the production of Web pages. This is a complex task. It involves creating a timetable that records the production of each content element of every Web page. Figure 7.5 is part of one such development timetable.

Stage 6: Finalization and Web Site Testing

Three weeks before releasing the Web site to students (stage 8), the process of requesting reproduction rights for copyrighted material stops. Although the requests would have been sent months before (stage 3), it is likely that some replies still have not been received. These cases need to be identified and the elements replaced.

In stage 6 the project manager

- stops the requests for reproduction rights;
- stops the development of Web pages; and
- ensures that the course Web site is ready for testing.

At this stage the site is finalized and no changes are made until after testing.

Testing the Web Site

This is the final opportunity for team members to review the Web pages and it is the first opportunity to test the entire site, focusing on ensuring that all elements are integrated. The content writer, educational designer, and Web designer meet and look at every Web page, making notes about

Web page header:	Topic 6.1: The Operating Environment		
Is the page part of prototype?	YES / **(NO)**		
Content storyboard developed?	**(YES)**/ NO	**Storyboard reviewed?**	**(YES)** / NO
Element	**Developed?**	**Any changes after page review?**	**Changes made?**
Text elements	Yes	No	—
Diagram of 4 parts of Operating Environment	Yes	Yes	Yes
Self-exercise (drag-and-drop type)	Yes	Yes	Yes
Accuracy of Kong (99) quote checked?	Yes	No	—
Web page header:	Subtopic 6.1.3: Suppliers		
Is the page part of prototype?	YES / **(NO)**		
Content storyboard developed?	**(YES)** / NO	**Storyboard reviewed?**	**(YES)** / NO
Element	**Developed?**	**Any changes after page review?**	**Changes made?**
Text elements	Yes	Yes	Yes
Photo of fresh food suppliers to hotel	Yes	No	—
Something to think about: Hilton Hotel suppliers	Yes	Yes	Yes
Self-exercise (multiple-choice)	Yes	No	—

FIGURE 7.5. An Extract from the Tracking Timetable for Content Element Production for the Strategic Management Web Site, Developed in the HTM Project

- essential changes;
- desirable changes; and
- aspects that could be improved in a future version.

This testing involves using the Web site on a variety of computers, ranging from those with the minimum hardware and software requirements to those exceeding the recommended requirements. Once testing is complete, the project manager organizes for the essential changes to be made. If time allows, the desirable changes are also made. Otherwise they wait until the site undergoes a maintenance or revision process.

Stage 7: Writing the Course Outline

The content writer, teacher, and educational designer write the course outline (Topic 4.5). This document introduces students to the teacher, the content, the requirements for successful course completion, and the learning resources. The information that should be in an outline about a course Web site includes

- its Web address;
- the minimum and recommended computer configurations;
- whether students need a username and password;
- why students should use the site;
- how the teacher expects students to use the site; and
- how students can expect the teacher to use the site.

Stage 8: Web Site Release

To ensure that the release of a Web site is a success, students need to be aware of its existence and able to access it.

Advertising

There should be a plan for making students aware of a course Web site, its features, and how it can help them. Sometimes a site is not used because not enough people know about it. In the rush to finish production, the need to advertise can be overlooked. Methods to make students aware of a Web site include

- demonstrating the site to students at the start of semester;
- the teacher referring to and using the site;
- explaining the site in the course outline;
- placing notices around the school; and
- distributing bookmarks containing the Web site address and an explanation of the access procedure.

Access

I advocate that the access policy for course Web sites be determined on a case-by-case basis. This is in contrast to a universal policy imposed on all institutional sites regardless of the different roles of sites and the wishes of team members. Too often sites are locked away and access restricted in the belief that they are the jewels of an institution. As discussed in Topic 1.2, teachers rather than Web sites

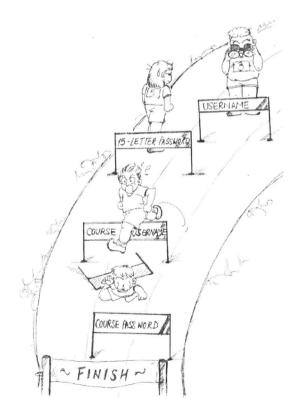

are the jewels. Unnecessary access restrictions can make maximizing the return on investment difficult.

If the decision is made to restrict access, it then needs to be decided whether each student will require a unique username and password. The following are recommendations about restricting access by using usernames and passwords:

- If students can contribute to a Web site, for example in a computer-mediated environment, then each student should have a unique username and password. The ability to identify who has posted information to a site is a legal requirement in many countries.
- If each student is provided with a unique username and password, they should be used for all course Web sites the student is allowed to access. Many course management systems support such an approach.
- If the teacher is the only person who can post to or modify information on a site, then unique usernames and passwords for students may not be necessary.
- If the desire to protect intellectual property rights is the main reason for wanting username and password protection, first consider what will be lost, as well as gained, by restricting access and the actual effectiveness of protection measures (Topic 4.6).

TOPIC 7.5: DESIGN

A design is applied to quality content to create a resource. The process described in Topic 7.4 of applying a design is called production. In this topic, the focus shifts to thinking about the design of course Web sites.

The complexity of a design depends on the amount of a course syllabus for which a resource is being developed. Although the examples used in this topic come from the HTM project, where Web sites for use as supplementary resources were developed for entire courses, my goal is to describe issues in a general way.

Ideally, every Web project would employ a professional Web designer. However, the reality is that in educational institutions Web design is often one of the roles of a teacher involved in the project, or an educational designer. Generally, such people use Web design software that does most of the computer coding for them and provides a range of Web site templates. It is people such as these that this topic aims to help. Items and events that are important in ensuring a good design specification include the following:

- Different people have different opinions of a design. You cannot satisfy all designers, teachers, and students. What is important is that you can explain how the design aims to help students understand the course.
- Finalize the design after deciding the minimum and recommended computer platforms.
- As you use the World Wide Web, make notes about designs you like and dislike.
- When designing a Web site, continually ask yourself this question: "As students use the site, can they easily determine where they are in the site, where they have been, and where they can go?"
- A Web site does not have to contain interactive activities, such as simulations, to be an effective learning resource.
- Design accessible Web sites that are based on a recognition that not all students can see, hear, and touch as well as others.
- There are differences between the design of course Web sites and those that businesses create for marketing and e-commerce purposes. Therefore, not all design guidelines for business sites apply to course sites.
- A design specification can be altered as the skills and experiences of team members develop.
- A design is a balance between consistency and variety. Consistency is required to help students use a resource. Variety is needed to motivate students and help them understand course content.
- When in doubt, ask some colleagues and students for their opinions. Informal small-scale surveys are a quick way of refining a design.

The Elements of a Web Site

Figures 7.6 and 7.7 are two Web pages created during the HTM Project for the strategic management site. They consist of Web ele-

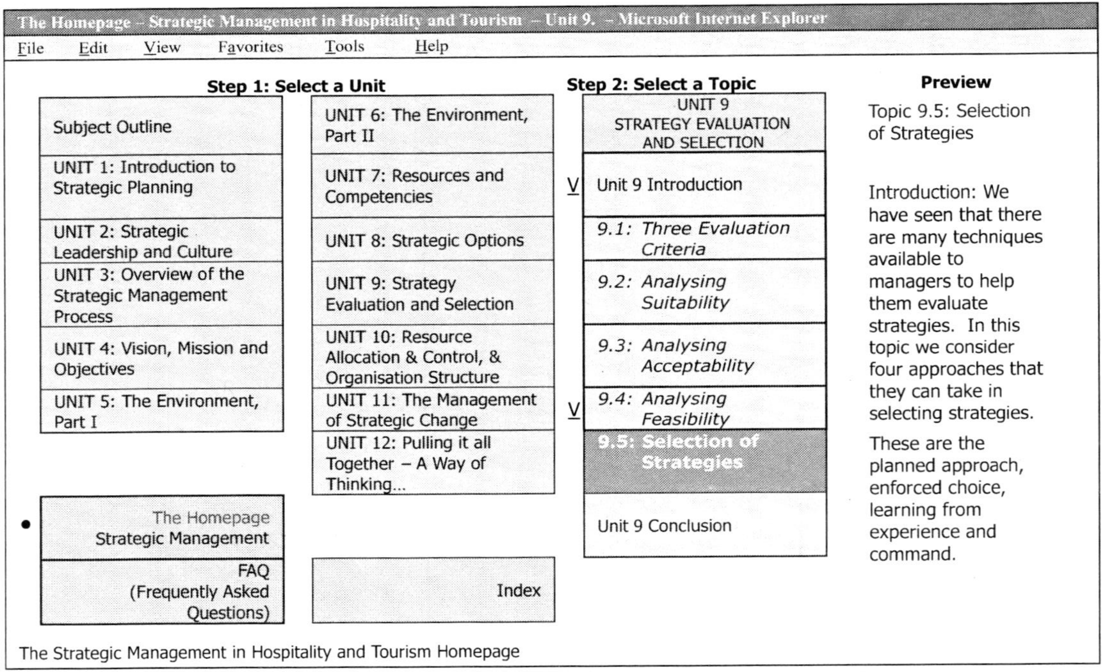

FIGURE 7.6. The Home Page for the Strategic Management Web Site, Developed in the HTM Project (*Source:* Reproduced with permission from the Strategic Management flexible learning package. The School of Hotel and Tourism Management at The Hong Kong Polytechnic University, Hong Kong.)

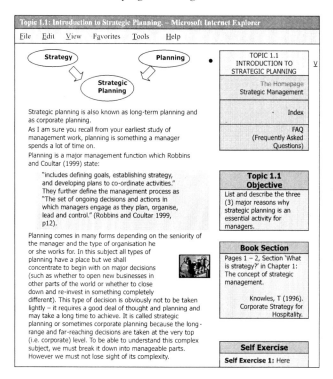

FIGURE 7.7. A Web Page from the Strategic Management Web Site, Developed in the HTM Project (*Source:* Reproduced with permission from the Strategic Management flexible learning package, The School of Hotel and Tourism Management at The Hong Kong Polytechnic University, Hong Kong.)

ments that are referred to throughout this topic. There are two types of elements:

1. *Navigation elements* provide the infrastructure associated with answering these questions: Where am I? Where can I go? What have I seen? These are the elements produced in stage 4, "Establishing the Web Site Shell" of the production process (Topic 7.4).
2. *Content elements* are the building blocks for course content. They help answer these questions: Why am I using this resource? How does this relate to my world? How can I determine

if I understand? What do other people think? These are produced in stage 5 of the production process.

The Minimum and Recommended Computer Platforms

The main factors that influence the design of a course Web site are
the needs, wants, and technology of students (Topic 5.3). Teacher, institution, and course factors also have an effect (Topic 5.4). These
factors, along with the general telecommunications infrastructure, influence the types of activities developed. For example, simulations
involving the production of video and animation elements may be appropriate from an educational perspective, but not feasible given the
types of computers students can access and the lack of a broadband
communications infrastructure.

Therefore a team needs to decide early in a project what the minimum and recommended computer platforms for using the Web site
will be. A computer platform consists of hardware and software. All
parts of a Web site should work on the minimum platform, while the
recommended platform allows "ideal" use of the site. For example, a
Web site that includes video clips may have a minimum platform that
specifies a 56K-modem Internet connection and a recommended
platform that includes a broadband quality connection.

Interactivity and Web Sites

Too many Web projects focus on building the equivalent of palaces
when houses would be sufficient. This is partly because some people
are overly critical of sites that are not interactive and do not use the
latest design techniques. Laurillard (1993) described interactivity as
"involving intrinsic feedback on what the student does—the information in the system should change as a result of their [students'] action" (p. 117). Such feedback is the defining characteristic of interactive activities. For example, a simulation of a restaurant business in
which students alter the types and relative values of costs and see the
effects on the gross operating profit is an interactive activity.

An emphasis on including interactive activities is appropriate in
sites that function as core learning resources. However, they are not
the only way of transmitting information and helping students. Other
learning opportunities involving the use of text, graphics, photos,
sound, video, and animations are also appropriate. For example, in

the Web page shown in Figure 7.7, a simple diagram, a highlighted quote, an animation of people playing chess, and text are used to convey information about strategic planning. The majority of course Web sites use such methods. Therefore, a project team must not feel that they have to include interactive exercises. Instead the objective is to design sites that help students and teachers.

Why Am I Using This Resource?

This section and the following four are about applying the general educational guidelines described in Topic 4.4 to Web sites. The equivalent sections of Topic 6.4 are also relevant as many of the techniques applicable to designing print resources also apply to Web sites.

Learning objectives are important in helping students remember why they are using a resource. In a Web site, objectives can be emphasized in the following ways:

- Objectives relevant to the content of a Web page can appear on the page and be emphasized in a *highlighted box*. For example, in Figure 7.7 the Topic 1.1 objective is a highlighted box.
- A self-exercise that focuses on testing a student's ability to achieve the learning objectives can act as an *advanced organizer* when placed at the start of the relevant section of a Web site.

Where Am I? Where Can I Go? What Have I Seen?

Designing the structure of a Web site involves challenges different than those faced when developing a print resource. A print resource is a physical item. You can hold it and see all its parts as you flip through its pages. In contrast, you cannot see all of a Web site at the same time. You can be told it contains seventy-three pages, but you cannot see all of those pages at once, and as soon as you move to a new page, the current page disappears. It is difficult to get a sense of the dimensions of a Web site. This can be discomforting and confusing.

As well, the control that a student can have over a Web site can cause difficulties. Generally when using computer programs, the weaker a student's prior knowledge of course content, the less benefit will be derived from student control. A reason for this is that the ability to make appropriate decisions such as the content to visit, the content sequence, the activities to select, and when and how to use them is not adequately developed (Gall and Hannafin, 1994; Atkins, 1993; Viau and Larivée, 1993; Ross and Morrison, 1989; Hammond and Allinson, 1988). Therefore, it is important to have an implied sequence of Web pages. For example, in Figure 7.6 the arrangement of the navigational buttons for the units, top to bottom and left to right, implies a sequence, as does the sequence, top to bottom, and numbering of the Unit 9 topics. However, a student still has control over the sequence of units and topics. The implied recommended order does not have to be followed. An implied sequence is also evident in Figure 7.2.

The following are issues and techniques about designing a navigational structure to help students answer these questions: Where am I? Where can I go? What have I seen?

- *Navigational buttons have consistent styles, functions, and locations.* This helps students identify sections and understand the relationships among them. For example, consider the navigational buttons shown in Figures 7.2 and 7.7. The buttons have consistent styles, with three buttons ("The Homepage Strategic Management," "Index," and "FAQ") in a different color than that used for topic and subtopic buttons. The functions of the buttons and their locations are also consistent. The consistency in style and function is also evident in Figure 7.6.
- Define one Web page as a site's *home page* and provide a link to this on all pages (Figure 7.6).
- To help students make informed decisions about what parts of a Web site to visit, *content previews* can be used. For example, in Figure 7.6 a preview is shown for Topic 9.5: Selection of Strategies. A student sees this while placing the computer mouse over the topic button. Having read the description, the student can choose to visit that section or select another preview.
- At the top of each Web page, have a *header* that identifies the page. For example, in Figure 7.6 the header is "The Homepage—Strategic Management in Hospitality and Tourism—Unit 9," while in Figure 7.7, the header is "Topic 1.1: Introduction to Strategic Planning."

- *Visual clues* can indicate which parts of a Web site have been visited and which section is currently on screen. For example, in Figures 7.6 and 7.7 the underlined letter v̲ indicates sections already visited, while the dot appears next to the section that is currently on screen.
- An *index* page can provide a list of all pages, with different colors indicating visited and nonvisited sections.
- A *search facility* can allow students to use keywords to identify and visit specific sections of a Web site.

How Does This Relate to My World?

The two techniques, "something to think about" sections and mentioning local businesses, discussed in the corresponding section for the design of print resources in Topic 6.4 also apply to Web sites. These can be enhanced in sites by using

- photos;
- links to business Web sites; and
- video movies and audio files to present examples of local businesses and the opinions of industry practitioners.

A characteristic of a "something to think about" section is that it finishes with questions to prompt students to evaluate their understandings and to encourage debate. With Web sites, debate can be encouraged by providing an electronic discussion space, such as a Web forum or Listserv (Chapter 8).

How Can I Determine If I Understand?

Self-exercise activities are a way of helping students determine the extent of their understandings of course content. Topic 4.4 contains a discussion about these exercises, including issues to think about and a description of what makes a good exercise.

In a Web site, self-exercise activities can be built using many different elements such as textual descriptions, photos, diagrams, video, audio, and animations. In Figure 7.7 part of a highlight box for a self-exercise appears in the right column. The exercise itself appears further down the Web page. The purpose of the box is to draw the attention of students to the exercise. By selecting a link in the box, the student can go directly to the exercise.

Common types of exercises used in course Web sites are *drag-and-drop, true/false,* and *multiple-choice.* Templates for these are in most course management systems (Chapter 9). With *rollover* exercises a student is asked to think about an answer to a question and decides when to rollover, that is, place the mouse over a part of the Web page, to see the answer.

Predict-observe-explain simulations are another type of self-exercise. A student experiments by

- reading a description of a situation and predicting what will occur when a specific change is made;
- altering the situation, for example, by changing the value of a variable and observing the effect; and
- explaining the result by either confirming that it matches the prediction or attempting to resolve any differences by conducting more experiments.

What Do Other People Think?

To help students develop their understandings, it is important to provide them with opportunities to

- discuss matters with their fellow students and the teacher;
- hear and read about the experiences of industry-based people; and
- realize that experts have differing views.

The techniques described in the corresponding section of Topic 6.4 about print resources can also be used in Web sites. For example, *discussion points* can be linked directly to a computer-mediated contact environment, such as a Web forum; *direct links to Web sites* can encourage students to visit the sites; and relevant pages of a textbook can be emphasized in a "book section" *highlight box,* as shown in Figure 7.7.

Also, a course Web site can include the following types of activities to help students experience what other people think:

- *Video movies* and *audio files* where other teachers and industry-based practitioners describe their opinions and experiences

- *Integration with electronic libraries* involving direct links to articles recommended by the teacher
- Inclusion of *links to online newspapers and radio stations* to help students gain a better understanding of cultures and lifestyles

Video and Audio in Course Web Sites

As more students have access to Internet-enabled computers with fast network connections, the inclusion of video movies, consisting of both audio and video, and audio files in course Web sites is increasing. The first step for a project team is to consider from an educational perspective why such activities should be developed. The second step involves producing the activities. The production process involves recording, digitizing, editing, optimizing, and delivering video movies and audio files on the basis of a variety of design and technical decisions, such as

- achieving a balance between size and quality of the video movie or audio file;
- whether bandwidth negotiation will be used so that the Web server interrogates the student's computer in order to deliver the optimum video movie or audio file;
- whether activities will play in a streaming, pseudostreaming, or nonstreaming manner;
- whether activities will play within Web pages or open in a new window; and
- the extent of student control to be provided over the way the video movie or audio file plays.

The technical issues and process of producing such activities are matters that need to be discussed with Web designers and programmers. This section focuses on the first step of considering the situations, from an educational perspective, where such activities may assist flexible learning students in understanding course content. The following are situations in which to consider producing such activities.

When a Simulation of a Real-Life Situation Can Help Develop Understanding

Video movies can be a powerful complement to textual and pictorial descriptions commonly included in Web pages. For example, student actors and a teacher can be involved in simulating a restaurant environment where the learning objective is to understand the moments of truth, both good and bad, in service encounters and how to make them into moments of magic. The actors can simulate parts of the service encounter, such as greeting customers and taking food orders, with the teacher interspersing the simulation with comments referring to parts of the accompanying textual description on the Web page.

To Provide Lecture Video Movies or Audio Files of a Teacher

Providing video movies or audio files of a teacher explaining course concepts is a contentious issue among educationalists. It can be seen as using the medium of the Internet purely as a means of continuing existing teaching practices, in this case the on-campus lecture, and in the process not considering how best to use the Internet to help students. I agree with this view when a lecture movie or audio file is placed on a course Web site as a continuous thirty- or sixty-minute activity with no integration with other content, and the recording was made by placing a camera with a wide-angle focus at the back of an on-campus lecture. However, lecture movies and audio files of the course teacher do have potential to be useful learning aids when guidelines such as the following are applied:

- If an on-campus lecture is video recorded, a skilled operator needs to vary the focus of the camera between the teacher, any slides and writing on whiteboards, and the students. The video needs to be more than a wide-angle perspective with the teacher indistinguishable in the distance.
- Unless it is important for conceptual understanding to see the teacher, an audio file should be developed in preference to a video movie. Such audio-only files are usually smaller than video movies and therefore allow more efficient delivery via the Internet.

- Produce a series of video movies or audio files rather than one continuous activity. For example, instead of having a fifty-minute lecture video, divide it into ten-minute segments, each accessible from a separate link on a Web page.
- Integrate video movie segments and audio segments into a course Web site. For example, a course may have a Web site where students can access textual and pictorial notes that are arranged on a topic-by-topic basis over a number of pages. Distribute the segments over the related pages and with each link provide an overview of what the video movie or audio file is about. This will help students make informed decisions about whether to select each segment.

To Introduce the Course and Teacher

A short video movie at the start of a course Web site can be a useful way of introducing the teacher. At the same time, the movie can help explain essential course requirements and how to use the site.

When Seeing an Environment and Hearing an Accompanying Description Can Help Develop Understanding

In courses designed to help students understand and work in a global environment, video movies showing contexts and cultures different from theirs can be useful learning resources. For example, a video illustrating the differences between restaurants in Sydney, Australia, and Hong Kong, China, in regard to the design of external and internal environments could be used in hospitality management courses in both countries. Such a video could be integrated with photos, textual descriptions, and activities on the course Web site to provide an in-depth study of restaurant design. In addition, after viewing the same video, students from both countries could debate issues using a computer-mediated contact tool, such as a Web forum (Chapter 8).

To Experience the Views of Industry Practitioners

In flexible learning courses with no on-campus classes, it can be challenging to provide opportunities for students to hear directly from industry practitioners. Audio-based interviews can be one way of providing such opportunities. Recording such interviews is technically a simple process and the small file sizes, compared to video movies, facilitate integration of the interviews into Web pages that include related content.

General Web Design Issues

Previous sections of this topic focused on the educational aspects of designing Web sites. In this final section the focus shifts to providing some general design guidelines:

- *Consistency in a Web site.* Consistency in functionality and style is important. For example, if you decide that all links to World Wide Web sites will open in a new browser window and internal links will open in the existing window, the rule must apply all the time.
- *Consistency among Web sites.* When developing more than one Web site, consistency in functionality is more important than consistency in style. For example, the font and colors used in a home page button can differ between sites, but the button must always link to a site's home page.
- *Design accessible Web sites.* Design so that students with characteristics such as imperfect vision and hearing can use the course Web site. By consulting with a design specialist, you can avoid unnecessary barriers for students, such as:
  a. navigational buttons that are small and difficult for someone with imperfect hand-eye coordination or vision;
  b. audio files that do not include the option of simultaneously reading a transcript; and
  c. frame-based page layouts that may cause difficulties for screen readers used by people with imperfect vision.
- *Keep documentation.* Keep all notes created during the design process. A design is a work in progress, and ideas initially dismissed may ultimately prove useful.
- *Be willing to integrate media other than the Internet.* Not all activities can be, nor should be, completed using a computer. Often the best teaching and learning environments involve a variety of learning opportunities using a range of media. Consider asking students to complete some activities on paper and include print-friendly activity sheets.

- *Printing.* Most likely, students will want to print out some pages. Therefore, consider providing printer-friendly versions of important pages.
- *Use design standards.* Although Web design principles are still evolving, some already exist that should be followed. For example, blue is the color for a link yet to be selected while red represents a link already selected.
- *Use color.* Although using color in print resources is expensive due to printing costs, this is not an issue with Web sites. Base a site's color palette on an understanding of color blindness, particularly the most common type, red-green color blindness, where distinguishing between shades of red and green is difficult.
- *What is not on a Web page is as important as what is.* Reading large amounts of text on computer screens is more difficult than on paper. Therefore, text needs to be adequately spaced and sized. A balance needs to be achieved between text, images, and empty space.

TOPIC 7.6: MAINTENANCE AND REVISION

Maintenance involves making small changes to any combination of the quality content (Topic 4.3), the design (Topic 7.5), and the production process (Topic 7.4). It usually relates to time-dependent matters. For example, Web site addresses change and it is necessary to regularly check them. Revision involves making larger changes. For example, following the use of a course Web site, a teacher may conclude that a particular self-exercise confused some students and may have caused them to misunderstand certain course concepts. Redesigning this exercise would be part of a revision process.

A Web site should undergo a maintenance program just before a course is taught. A revision process should occur at least once every two years. Although an educational designer or project assistant can complete most maintenance requirements, revision also requires the commitment of a content writer and a Web designer. A Web programmer will also be involved if complex programming is necessary. The following are questions to ask and issues to consider about maintaining and revising a Web site, in addition to those discussed in Topic 6.5 that are relevant to Web sites as well as print resources.

Maintenance Issues

- Are all links to Web sites working and is the content still relevant?
- To what extent do Web pages work when viewed on recently released versions of Web browsers? If some Web elements do not work, a revision process may be necessary.
- Despite comprehensive testing during the production process, some Web elements may not work on particular computer configurations. By maintaining a diary, teachers can document the problems identified by students and tell a Web designer about the problems.
- The problem of students and teachers using different versions of a Web site does not usually occur as only one version exists on a Web server. However, multiple versions can occur if a site is duplicated, that is, "mirrored," on other servers or if the site is also distributed on a CD-ROM. The project manager is responsible for maintaining and distributing the most recent version.

Revision Issues

- Changes to the content may be necessary after the teacher and students have used the Web site. These changes can be significant. For example, as a result of marking students' examination papers, a teacher may conclude that most students did not develop a sufficient understanding of an important concept. In order to help future students, it may be necessary to make major changes to the site. This will involve the development of new Web elements and therefore involve a content writer, an educational designer, a Web designer, and possibly a Web programmer.
- The field of course Web site design and use is less than twenty-five years old. Therefore, our understanding continues to rapidly evolve. A revision process should include consideration of the applicability of recent technical advances and research findings.

- Once all changes have been made to Web pages, the integrity of all internal links should be checked. Revisions may have resulted in entire pages, or parts of pages, being deleted.

KEY POINTS

1. By acting as Web advisors, teachers can help students use the World Wide Web

   - as a source of information to help them understand course concepts;
   - to develop their general Internet skills; and
   - to develop an awareness of the applications of the Internet to the industry they are learning about.

2. A good Web site design is one that you can justify by explaining how it aims to help students understand a course and how it is based on design standards.
3. When you are developing a course Web site, access it from computers of friends and from Internet cafés. Doing this throughout the production process will remind you of the variety in computer configurations and how a site that works on your computer may not look as good or work as well on other systems.

Chapter 8

Computer-Mediated Contact

Computer-mediated contact (CMC) tools, such as e-mail, Web forums, and Listservs, can be useful in on-campus and off-campus learning and teaching environments.

Online communities are enhanced by the involvement of teachers who use teaching, social, and managerial strategies to nurture and maintain debates and discussions. A training and support structure, which focuses on both technical and educational issues, helps students and teachers make the most of CMC environments.

OBJECTIVES

1. To explain what CMC is and the advantages and challenges it offers teachers and students
2. To recommend that teachers participate in CMC environments by making original postings, replying to postings, and summarizing discussions
3. To list and explain teaching, social, and managerial strategies that teachers can use to maintain an effective online community throughout the semester
4. To describe the training and support structure, for both teachers and students, necessary for a successful CMC environment

TOPIC 8.1: INTRODUCTION

CMC involves using the Internet to send and receive messages.

This chapter is particularly relevant to teachers and educational designers. It focuses on the educational aspects of CMC.

- In Topic 8.1 the types of CMC are described.
- In Topic 8.2 the advantages and challenges for students and teachers when using CMC environments are considered.
- Topic 8.3 focuses on teaching and learning strategies, which range across the spectrum of teacher-student interaction, from one-on-one to many-to-many.
- Topic 8.4 is about the training and support infrastructure necessary to ensure that CMC is a valued part of learning and teaching environments.

Too often, CMC environments are like shooting stars in the night sky. They appear in a blaze of publicity in the first week of the semester, are used for a few weeks, and then rapidly fade away. The goal of this chapter is to help you ensure that CMC occurs throughout the semester.

The students' voices that appear throughout this chapter are those of undergraduate and postgraduate distance education students, who had access to course Web forums as described in Williams (2001).

Types of Computer-Mediated Contact

CMC can be synchronous or asynchronous. The defining characteristic of synchronous communication is that it occurs in close to real time, with minimal delay between the time when a message is sent and when it is read. The sender and receiver are connected to the Internet at the same time. Many course management systems (Chapter 9) include synchronous tools, some of which allow participants to draw on electronic whiteboards as well as typing messages to each other.

In contrast, the defining characteristic of asynchronous communication is a delay between the time when a message is sent and when it is read. The sender and receiver do not have to be connected to the Internet at the same time. Three common asynchronous CMC tools are e-mail, Listservs, and Web forums:

1. E-mail is the most popular form of asynchronous communication.
2. In a Listserv, a person participates after a moderator has accepted a request to subscribe. Participants e-mail messages to a Listserv address, and the messages are automatically e-mailed to all subscribers.
3. A Web forum is based upon the World Wide Web. Messages are read, sent, and archived using a Web browser and involve the participant navigating through the discussion using skills inherent to Web sites.

TOPIC 8.2: THE ADVANTAGES AND CHALLENGES OF COMPUTER-MEDIATED CONTACT

Often CMC is seen as something useful in flexible learning environments, but of little use when students attend regular face-to-face classes. However, CMC can occur in most learning environments. For example, when an on-campus lecture ends, students' understandings are likely to be incomplete. CMC environments can facilitate the process of making sense. For example, after a lecture, a teacher can place some questions and further information about the lecture content on a Web forum.

Therefore, many of the advantages and challenges of CMC apply across the range of learning and teaching environments. However, in an environment with no regular face-to-face contact, CMC is more likely to be a core learning resource. This is in comparison to a weekly on-campus environment, where CMC is likely to be a supplementary resource, supporting core resources such as lectures and tutorials.

Advantages of Computer-Mediated Contact

Advantages of CMC environments for students include the following:

- Students can receive additional information from the teacher and their fellow students about concepts they are having difficulty understanding. One student commented:

  It was good to see where other people were having problems and their solutions. By using the forum I could avoid making, or easily resolve, common mistakes.

- A curriculum is often crowded as the teacher balances the need to complete the syllabus with the desire to help students. Opportunities to discuss the formal content of a course and also life experiences and work-based activities related to the course are usually limited. A CMC environment can be used to facilitate such discussions (Rowntree, 1995). Such real-life experiences help many students assimilate and accommodate information.
- Participating in an online discussion group can help students experience the real-world situation of offering an idea, receiving critiques, and, in light of others' views, sometimes modifying their beliefs. This aspect of CMC is particularly important for students that rarely, if ever, attend face-to-face tutorials in which teachers often encourage such discussions.
- A CMC environment can be used to support consideration of content beyond that included in the course syllabus. Concepts

can be discussed that are not part of the course. Also, concepts can be explored to a deeper level than that required to pass the course.

- Asynchronous CMC environments support students who want to contribute to discussions but prefer to first reflect upon what other people have written.
- Feelings of isolation can be reduced through being part of an online community. This is particularly applicable to students who rarely, if ever, see their fellow students and teachers. One student noted:

I found the forum to be an extremely useful outlet for contact with other students. One of the hardest parts of distance education, if you are struggling, is knowing if others are as well. It helped to improve my self-confidence knowing that others had problems in the same areas as me. It is also useful to know if you are on the right track with the subject or not. I rate this as the most valuable part of the online package.

CMC environments can help teachers in the following ways:

- CMC can reduce the need for teachers to deal with the same question or problem over and over again. An asynchronous environment, such as a Web forum or Listserv, can be used to post answers to frequently asked questions. A weekly e-mail to students is another way of distributing information.
- Reading students' contributions to CMC environments can help teachers develop their awareness of the needs and lives of students.
- Contact between a student and a teacher is greatly facilitated by e-mail. Providing personalized help, such as in-depth feedback about an assignment, can be difficult and inappropriate in group settings such as tutorials. Sending an e-mail is a quick and relatively secure way of teacher-to-student communication.
- By observing and participating in a CMC environment, teachers can extend their knowledge of course content. For example, students may post information about Web sites they have found useful. These sites, and the associated online debate among students and teachers, can help develop everyone's understandings.

Challenges of Computer-Mediated Contact

Many of the challenges of CMC relate to the fact that the environment is new for many students and teachers:

- Verbal and visual clues are lacking in an online environment. For example, in a face-to-face situation a teacher will adjust the presentation in response to visual clues from students. Such clues are lacking in a CMC environment.
- All participants in an online discussion need to be able to analyze a posting and phrase questions so as to get answers. Guidance and practice about how to write an effective message is often necessary.
- Students and teachers who use e-mail can suffer from asynchronous anxiety. A common symptom is phoning a person to check that an e-mail has been received. For example, a student who sends an e-mail may worry that the teacher has not received it, because five hours have passed and no response has been received. Reducing this anxiety involves developing a trusting environment for participants. Teachers can reduce this anxiety among students by explicitly stating how frequently they will read and respond to messages. A student who knows a teacher will aim to reply within two days is less likely to be anxious than one who is unaware of the teacher's policy.
- Time management skills are important. A CMC environment is another resource to think about in an already busy day. Techniques such as checking e-mail only twice daily and filtering e-mails into course-specific folders should be used.
- Financial costs are associated with CMC environments and teachers need to consider whether it is appropriate to expect students to pay. These costs include not only the computer, but also the costs of an Internet service provider and phone calls. In some countries, calls are charged on a timed basis. Before expecting students to be online for a one-hour synchronous chat, a teacher needs to consider the costs and benefits carefully.
- To create a CMC community, people must post messages. Many CMC environments promoted as useful learning resources fail because of nonparticipation by students and teachers. Teachers commented:

No one used it. It seems a waste, as I thought it was a very good idea. Maybe none of the students have Internet access?

Unfortunately there were not many students who actually used the forum so I found it of little use.

- Teachers and students need to learn how to use applications such as Web browsers and e-mail programs.

TOPIC 8.3: TEACHERS' ROLES

As a distance education student one often feels isolated. The forum has enabled me to feel as though I am part of a group and involved. The questions other students ask are of real interest to me (it is nice to know other students get confused too!). The feedback from the lecturer is extremely valuable.

This theme of this topic is that effective CMC environments depend on learning experiences that are structured and facilitated by teachers. The topic is based upon the work of Williams (1997, 2001) and is written for teachers.

While I was involved in the establishment and nurturing of CMC environments, I developed a list of best practices based upon observing teachers who have integrated CMC into course curricula:

- *Explicitly tell students how you will be involved.* At the start of the semester, make it clear how you will be involved in the CMC environment. State your intentions in a document, such as the course outline. For example, if you intend to reply to e-mails within two days, tell students this is your policy. If you plan to read contributions to a Web forum once a day, tell students that is what you will do. If you aim to be in the virtual chat room between ten o'clock and eleven o'clock every Tuesday night, tell them you will be there.
- *Practice what you preach—participate.* If you participate in discussions, it is more likely that students will also value the CMC environment and make postings.
- *Integrate the CMC environment into the course curriculum.* A CMC environment that is separate from the curriculum and is not explicitly used to help students understand the course is

likely to fail. Here are two examples about making it part of the everyday learning situation. For example:

    a. After a lecture, post some questions about the lecture content to a Web forum, which students can use to self-test their understandings.

    b. If you send a weekly e-mail to students studying away from your institution, include reminders about the part of the course students should be studying and provide guidance about particularly important concepts.

- *Be prepared to help students learn how to use the CMC tool.* Although you are not expected to be an expert on the technical aspects of using a CMC tool, you should be able to explain how to access the CMC environment and how to perform fundamental skills, such as reading and replying to messages.

The Teacher As Moderator

It was interesting. I was aided by fellow students. However, I would have preferred that the lecturer also participated in the online discussions more for accuracy purposes and perhaps as a stimulant. However, [he] walks the line/tightrope requiring [a] balance between putting [a] dampener on discussion and breaking open the subject for greater discussion.

CMC moderation *involves participation by a teacher in the nurturing and maintenance of the environment. Participation involves making original postings, replying to postings, summarizing discussions, and filtering inappropriate contributions.*

In the majority of situations, a teacher should moderate a CMC environment. The extent to which the teacher acts as a message filter varies. In a highly censored group, the teacher will read all messages before they are posted to students. Such intensive censoring is rarely necessary and is time consuming. Instead, the censoring role should be a minor part of CMC moderation compared to nurturing communication through participation in discussions.

Teaching Strategies

It gave an opportunity to share ideas, opinions, and ask for advice from fellow students. It was a very positive experience. It also gave us the opportunity to communicate with our lecturer . . . who responded promptly.

CMC teaching strategies involve the teacher as an educational facilitator. As a content expert, the teacher aims to help students develop their understandings.

These strategies will help teachers establish and maintain a CMC environment:

1. *Alert to argument:* Draw attention to opposing perspectives that could lead to debates.
2. *Any problems?* Every so often, post a message asking if anyone has any problems. It is best if this is asked in relation to specific course concepts. The question, "Does anyone have any problems with what we discussed last week?" is less likely to get a response than the following more directed question: "Last week we discussed quality service principles and their implications for front-of-house hotel staff. Does anyone have any problems with that topic?"
3. *Assessment:* Should you assess students' CMC contributions? There is no definitive answer to this question. Some teachers believe that you should not force students to participate. Others see assessment as rewarding efforts to understand and help other students. Assessing contributions is an art, not a science. The subjective nature of the process means that your assessment scheme can be broad and generous. I suggest that you do not count the number of words in each posting. Rather, assess the quality of each student's contributions to maintaining the CMC environment. If you choose to assess participation, make sure students understand the assessment criteria.
4. *Brainstorm:* Start a brainstorming session. You will need to state that all ideas, no matter how strange they seem, are encouraged and that people are not to criticize anyone's ideas. Good techniques to start such a session include asking a provocative question or expressing an unpopular opinion.
5. *Critique an article:* Provide guidelines about how to review articles and then ask a student, or a group of students, to review an article and post the review online. Then request that other students post their responses. Journal articles can be used. However, often the liveliest debates result from review-

ing newspaper articles. For example, as a result of a subway extension project, hoteliers may be calling for compensation due to a downturn in occupancy rates near the construction site. A group of students could review a newspaper article about this issue. The merits of the hoteliers' position can be discussed as well as strategies that could minimize any adverse effects.

6. *Cross-fertilization:* In courses that have both off-campus and on-campus students, a shared CMC environment can create opportunities for cross-fertilization of ideas between student groups. However, you must be alert to possible confusion caused by differing content schedules and assignments.

7. *Debate:* Conduct an online debate involving affirmative and negative sides. In your role of debate facilitator, you post the rules, such as the number of speakers and time per speaker, pose the issue, and at the end of the debate post a summary.

8. *False statement:* Post a deliberately misleading statement and encourage students to discover the false premise through discussion. Include in your posting a comment such as, "The following is based upon an invalid assumption. Discuss among yourselves my statements and see if you can identify the invalid assumptions." You need to carefully monitor the discussion. Make a posting at the end explicitly stating what was misleading and including the correct statements.

9. *Guests:* Invite a guest from industry to participate in a discussion. Students are asked to prepare questions. The guest can post some initial comments about an issue and then a question-and-answer session follows. This session can last minutes in a synchronous environment or weeks in an asynchronous situation. Guests are particularly valuable for students who do not attend on-campus classes. They can be a great way of exposing students to industry practitioners. For example, the human resources manager of a hotel can take part in a discussion, during a strategic human resources management course, on the challenges of maintaining a balance between employing local and expatriate managers.

10. *Hot seat:* Ask a student to "sit in the hot seat" and have other students ask questions on a specific topic for a specified length of time. You need to closely monitor such situations to

ensure an atmosphere of friendly questioning, rather than interrogation.

11. *Online poll:* Post a multiple-choice question and ask students to e-mail you their answers. You then post the result. Alternatively, some CMC tools include facilities for designing online polls that automatically collate and display results. Such polls can be a useful way of encouraging participation and provide ideal discussion prompts.

12. *Reactivating:* There will be times when few postings are made. For example, students can be busy with assignments or it can be midsemester break. It can be a challenge to get the discussion going again. In such a situation, you may need to phone or e-mail students and ask them to post messages about a controversial topic, thereby promoting reactivation of the discussion.

13. *Revisit:* Students move through course topics at different speeds. Therefore, it is important that you occasionally prompt a reexamination of a topic. A posting at the start of a course stating that everyone must accept that people work at different rates will help encourage students who fear posting to a discussion group because they think they have fallen behind. Prompts are useful when revisiting a topic. For example: "Remember how two weeks ago we had a guest—Mr. Leung— discuss the benefits of computer-based training in his organization? Let us now reflect on that discussion and list the potential benefits of such training."

14. *Rewording an ignored posting:* In a busy online discussion, a student's posting can be ignored. As moderator, you can repost the message and thereby encourage replies. For example: "Last week Kenith asked about the effectiveness of a government using the tax rate to encourage investment in new tourism ventures. Here are some of my thoughts about the merits of this idea. Does anyone have ideas to add?"

15. *Small-group work:* A CMC environment can help groups work together. For example, a course Web forum can contain a number of subforums accessible only to group members. In these "protected" environments, students collaborate. When a group has completed a task, they post a message containing the results of their work to the main forum.

16. *Student moderator:* Organize students to take over most of your moderator roles. For example, the student who is the moderator of the week will be responsible for posting summaries and encouraging students to post messages. Your role becomes that of a content expert, ensuring that misconceptions are recognized and corrected.

17. *Target a Web site:* An industry-relevant Web site can be the focus of an online discussion. You will need to design questions to encourage focused consideration of the site.

18. *Weaving:* The posting of messages to help students understand the flow of a discussion and its relationship to previous discussions is called weaving. As the moderator, you summarize discussions, identify themes, and help the online community achieve a sense of accomplishment and direction (Feenberg, 1989).

19. *Web site comparisons:* Use industry-based Web sites to help students learn about the applications of course concepts. To focus students, give them a task that involves comparing the information and approaches of a number of companies (see Exhibit 8.1).

EXHIBIT 8.1. CMC Teaching Strategies and Hotel and Tourism Management Courses

In the Hotel and Tourism Management School, I was involved in more than just the HTM Project. Another project was the implementation of a course management system so that every course had a Web site. Each site included a Web forum. As an educational technologist, a major part of my role was to encourage teachers to consider using the forums. The following are CMC teaching strategies I emphasized:

- *Critique an article:* The social and applied nature of the hospitality industry means that popular newspapers and magazines regularly include relevant articles and advertising. For example, the financial prospects of industry sectors are discussed in general business and economic magazines, and newspapers have supplements devoted to food and restaurant issues. Such materials can be the basis for critiquing an article.
- *Cross-fertilization* and *debates:* In many courses, the global nature of the industry, and consequently the importance of understanding cul-

(continued)

(continued)

tural issues, is emphasized. CMC environments can be used to allow students in different countries to compare and contrast their opinions. For example, in an events management course, students from past Olympic host cities can debate the advantages and disadvantages to the local communities of such major tourism events.

- *Guest:* Experiencing the views of industry practitioners enhances many hospitality courses. Both synchronous and asynchronous CMC environments can be used. The participants can be anywhere in the world. In asynchronous environments such as a Web forum, the conversation can occur over weeks as the guest speaker and students read and post messages at times they find convenient.

- *Target a Web site* and *Web site comparisons:* There are thousands of hospitality-based Web sites, and activities can make use of this information source. Activities should be highly structured, with explicit objectives, tasks, and instructions. For example: "Your task is to compare the mission statements for two companies, A and B, using our previously discussed quality criteria. For company A, the statement is available by following the links: Home Page > About the Company > Mission Statement. For company B, the statement is available by following the links: Home Page > Corporate Information > Quality Controls."

- *Online poll:* Hotel and tourism management is a topical and opinionated field of study. Some courses, such as financial management and quantitative methods for business, use widely accepted models and procedures. However, many other courses, such as strategic management and strategic marketing, have fewer universally accepted models and procedures. Online polls can be used to help students experience the diversity, or lack of diversity as the case may be, among their peers about course models, procedures, and implications. For example, during a discussion about reward structures to use in the workplace, a multiple-choice poll can be constructed for which students select the reward that they personally would most value. Once a student makes a choice, a graphic summary of the number of fellow students who have chosen each reward is shown. At the end of the polling period, a summary is placed in the CMC environment.

Social Strategies

CMC social strategies *are those involved with developing a CMC environment as a community of learners, rather than a group of individuals.*

Used it as a communication center with other students, asked for help, suggestions, and tried to offer help and assistance to other colleagues—often thought of it as a "discussion" time over a cup of tea in the uni café—without the café! Lecturer also involved though did not censor the conversation at all.

The following strategies will help teachers create an encouraging social environment for learners:

1. *Chatter:* Opinions as to the role of social chatter in a CMC environment vary. Some teachers want none, while others actively encourage it. I recommend that social chatter be allowed as it will encourage a sense of community. If such discussion begins to dominate, you can post a reminder of the main purpose of the CMC environment and suggest that social discussions continue by private e-mail.

2. *It is an online conversation, not a publication:* Encourage students to view posting a message as an act of speech, not an act of publishing. Therefore, although spelling and grammar should be correct, there is no need to prepare each posting as if it will be published in a book.

3. *Observers:* It is likely that some students will join a synchronous chat session or read asynchronous Web forum or Listserv messages but never post messages themselves. Part of your moderator role is to encourage such students to post. For example, you can phone them to check that a technical difficulty is not stopping them from posting. You can encourage observers to post messages by suggesting topics. However, accept that some people will always be observers, even when they lose marks because contributions form part of the course assessment. For some students, reading and listening are their preferred and effective learning strategies.

4. *Rudeness:* Do not ignore bad behavior. A student's posting may contain inappropriate language and comments about other students. In such cases, privately discuss the matter with the offender, contact victims to reassure them that their contributions are valued, and post to the CMC environment a reminder of the guidelines for contributing. Inappropriate messages can stifle participation, not only by those directly targeted but also by those wary of contributing. Therefore, you need to be prepared to act fast using a predetermined strategy that is consistently applied.

5. *Situated learning:* Relate course content to recent events. This will help in encouraging a sense of community and also help students understand the course concepts. A discussion in the first weeks of the semester about a local topic of interest to students is ideal for breaking down some of the barriers to establishing a community of learners.
6. *We are all learning:* As the teacher, maintain a nonauthoritarian style that recognizes that you and the students are learning how to use the CMC tools, and all participants are developing their understandings of the course. You are the content expert. There is no need to deny this fact. However, be prepared to be seen as uncertain about something and willing to find out. Students value such honesty.
7. *Who are you?* At the start of a course, post information about yourself to the CMC environment describing your professional and personal interests. Encourage students to also make such postings.
8. *Who's who?* If e-mail is the main CMC tool, consider distributing a list of students' e-mail addresses. However, before doing this, you must obtain permission from students to distribute their addresses.

Managerial Strategies

CMC managerial strategies *involve maintaining the day-to-day activities of a CMC environment.*

These strategies will help teachers manage a CMC environment:

1. *Check locations:* World Wide Web addresses, also known as universal resource locators (URLs), that are included in online discussions must be checked on a monthly basis. The Internet is constantly changing, and asking students to visit a location that no longer exists will cause frustration.
2. *Going away?* If you will not access the CMC environment for more than two days, let students know. Many CMC tools support the sending of an automatic response to a message, notifying the sender that you are away.

3. *No lecturing:* Remember that the longer the message, the harder it is to read, the more tedious it becomes, and the more likely it is to be ignored.

4. *Start with guidelines about contributing:* At the start of a course, post a message with guidelines. This explains to students the purpose of the CMC environment, your views on social chatter, and netiquette. The following are suggestions for netiquette guidelines:

  • Use a subject heading when you post a message. This heading helps your fellow students and the teacher follow the discussion. Do not use someone else's subject heading when you want to introduce a new topic.
  • When replying to a message, include only the parts of the original message you are replying to. Especially resist quoting someone else quoting a third person. Such messages are frustrating to read and most likely will be ignored.
  • Remember, the longer the message, the harder it is to read, the more tedious it becomes, and the more likely it will be ignored.
  • Use upper and lowercase text. Messages in all capital letters are the equivalent of shouting.
  • Remember that everyone studies at a different rate. Therefore, be tolerant of people posting messages about topics you have finished studying. Use your understanding to help your fellow students.
  • Be diplomatic. Criticism is always harsher when written. Read your message to yourself before you send it. So often we regret messages we send when we are angry, tired, busy, or feel strongly about something.
  • Stay calm. Remember, not everyone's computer skills are the same as yours, and everyone's English language skills are different.
  • Messages that inappropriately criticize people, attack people's personal beliefs, or contain unacceptable language will be removed. Penalties will be imposed in accordance with institutional regulations.

5. *You are the boss, not the computer:* You lead a busy life and there is no need to continually check for new postings to a Web forum or for e-mail messages. Tell students how often you will

check for messages and how soon you will reply. Discipline yourself to keep to this schedule. Recommend to students that they also adopt a schedule.

TOPIC 8.4: TRAINING AND SUPPORT ROLES

I have stated (Williams, 2001):

> In order to encourage use of cmc environments it is necessary to assist teachers and students in relation to two issues. There is the issue of technology literacy, for example: How to post a message to a web forum, and second, the issue of how to use the cmc environment to facilitate learning. (p. 115)

Training should be provided to teachers before the semester starts. For students, it should occur in the first weeks of the semester. A support infrastructure should exist throughout the course.

For both teachers and students, training opportunities and support should be offered using a variety of methods. For example, helping people with the technical aspects of using CMC tools can involve face-to-face workshops in a computer laboratory, paper handouts, Web-based tutorials, and access throughout the semester to people who can help.

Guidelines for Helping Teachers

The following are training and support guidelines for educational designers helping teachers use CMC environments.

Technical Issues

- Make sure that people explaining how to use CMC tools design their presentations to match the average technical literacy of the audience. Too often people leave presentations asking whether the presenter was from a different planet, because it was impossible to understand what was said.
- Training sessions should be held at least a month before the semester starts.
- CMC environments must be ready for teachers to use a month before semester starts. This allows teachers to experiment and learn in the context of their course Web sites.
- Ensure that throughout the semester a technical expert is available to help teachers in their offices. The expert should go to the teacher when requested rather than the teacher having to seek out the technical expert.

Educational Issues

- At least a month before the semester, give teachers documents describing what a CMC environment is, how it can help them teach, and strategies they can use.
- Hold workshops where teachers hear from experienced teachers about how they have integrated CMC into curricula. Often learning about the experiences of your colleagues is a powerful learning method. It is also useful if teachers can visit existing CMC course environments to see discussions in progress.

- Offer first-time CMC users the opportunity to have an experienced teacher as a mentor.
- Do not underestimate the commitment necessary to nurture a CMC environment. Teachers will ask, "Does moderating a CMC environment take lots of time and effort?" The answer is yes.

Guidelines for Helping Students

The following are training and support guidelines for teachers and educational designers in helping students use CMC environments:

Technical Issues

- Do not overestimate the technical literacy of students. Not every student is a computer expert.
- Hold training sessions during presemester orientation days. Otherwise the sessions should be held in the first weeks of the semester.
- Do not assume that because some students have already been at the institution for at least a year that they all know how to use the CMC tools. Offer refresher sessions that concentrate on recent changes.
- Students who are unsure how to use the fundamental features of a CMC environment, such as reading, sending, and replying to messages, should be able to ask their teachers for help. Teachers need to be able to answer such questions. Only if the issue is complex should it be necessary to suggest that the student contact a technical expert.

Educational Issues

- If there is a face-to-face lecture at the start of the semester, use the opportunity to demonstrate the CMC environment. This will ensure that students are aware of it, and it will show the value that the teacher places on it.
- Helping students use a CMC environment is an issue throughout the semester rather than something that can be handled in a

training session. The teacher needs to lead by example, using a wide variety of teaching, social, and managerial strategies.

- Ask students from the year ahead to explain how they used the CMC environment and the advantages and challenges of using it. Often people are more willing to use something once they have heard how it helped their peers.

KEY POINTS

1. CMC environments can be useful for students who attend campus weekly, as well as for flexible learning students who rarely, if ever, are on campus.
2. A CMC environment that is designed to help students understand a course involves the teacher as a participant. Students need and want teachers involved.
3. Participating in a CMC environment as a teacher takes time. However, the demands can be managed if students are explicitly made aware of how a teacher will participate.

Chapter 9

Course Management Systems

A course management system (CMS) facilitates an integrated approach to the development, use, and maintenance of course Web sites. Such systems can help teachers and students in on-campus courses, as well as flexible learning courses.

The success of a CMS depends on the training and support infrastructure. Once a CMS is either developed or purchased, the focus must be on the quality and effectiveness of course Web sites, rather than the number of visits to Web pages and the actions of competing institutions.

OBJECTIVES

1. To explain what CMSs are by describing their common features and uses, emphasizing that such systems can be used in on-campus, as well as off-campus, environments
2. To describe the advantages and challenges of a CMS from the perspectives of students, teachers, and institutions
3. To describe what needs to be considered when an institution is deciding whether to create or buy a CMS
4. To list factors teachers should consider before deciding to use a CMS
5. To emphasize the importance of a training and support structure, which includes how to use the software and hardware, and how to use the system for learning and teaching

TOPIC 9.1: INTRODUCTION

A ***course management system*** *(CMS) facilitates an integrated approach to the development, use, and maintenance of Web sites.*

More than thirty CMSs are commercially available, including products such as Blackboard, FirstClass, and WebCT. Such systems are widely used. For example, when a survey was distributed to forty-three Australian universities, the forty responding institutions all indicated that they used CMSs (Bell et al., 2002). Many reported using more than one system, and twenty reported using systems they had created.

Through a CMS, students can use Web sites developed by their teachers, including sites that support CMC. Therefore, Chapters 7 and 8 are also relevant if you are thinking about using a CMS.

Chapter 9 aims to help teachers, project managers, and educational designers make decisions about

- whether to use a CMS;
- whether to buy or create a system;
- how to use a system to help teachers teach and students learn; and
- the training and support infrastructure required to encourage effective use of a CMS.

The systems available from commercial vendors change as revisions are made and companies leave or enter the market. In this chapter different systems are not compared. Most course management systems

- facilitate the placing of materials online for access through an intranet, the Internet, or both;
- include synchronous and asynchronous communication tools;
- contain assessment tools and aids, such as quiz templates and assignment submission facilities; and
- have tools to help teachers monitor the progress of students and manage courses.

An ideal way of understanding the capabilities of a CMS is to experiment with one. The Web sites of commercial vendors have course Web sites you can visit.

When thinking about using a CMS, consider its potential usefulness to all students, regardless of the extent to which the environment is flexible. For example, I was involved in implementing a CMS to provide supplementary resources to students who attended weekly on-campus lectures and tutorials (see Exhibit 9.1). I was also involved in an implementation of a system for use by students who never saw their teachers or fellow students, and the CMS was used to provide core resources.

TOPIC 9.2: THE ADVANTAGES AND CHALLENGES OF COURSE MANAGEMENT SYSTEMS

This topic focuses on the advantages and challenges CMSs offer students, teachers, and institutions. Whether something is seen as an advantage or challenge depends on the context in which the system is used, including the skills of the people involved.

Students' Perspectives

In this topic, the assumption is that your school has decided to develop course Web sites and that the decision to be made is whether to use a CMS. First, the advantages and challenges of course management systems are considered from the student's perspective.

Advantages

- Usually, each course Web site has a similar design and functionality. Therefore, once students know how to use one site, they know how to use others.
- Many CMSs have a common gateway, also called a portal, which allows access to all courses a student is enrolled in from one Web page, using one username and password.

EXHIBIT 9.1. A Course Management System in a Hotel and Tourism Management School

This case study introduces the CMS implementation that is described in greater detail in Williams (2003). Although this implementation occurred in the same school as the HTM Project (Topic 1.3), it was a separate project.

Rationale

The teaching and learning committee of a hotel and tourism management school, in a Hong Kong university, used a CMS to provide supplementary learning resources for on-campus courses. The core resources for each course were on-campus weekly lectures and tutorials. The majority of the courses were for undergraduate students.

It was an ideal time for the school to implement a CMS:

- The university had recently purchased a commercial product for use as the preferred institution-wide CMS, and a maintenance and support infrastructure existed.
- University senior management emphasized the importance of schools exploring the potential of Internet and intranet networks to support teaching. Management wanted a return on the investment. Therefore, it was an opportunity to be seen as a proactive school supporting the university's strategies.

The Features of a Course Web Site

Every undergraduate and postgraduate course had a Web site. This meant there were fifty-five course sites each semester. The same template, containing the following five areas, was used in each Web site:

1. *Calendar*—where the teacher could indicate important events, such as assignment due dates and changes to the lecture schedule
2. *Course Materials*—an area where the teacher could make available supplementary materials, such as PowerPoint presentations and additional reading lists
3. *Communication Tools*—an asynchronous Web forum, a private mail facility, and synchronous chat and whiteboard facilities
4. *Assessment Tools*—where a teacher could create quizzes and electronic assignment submission boxes
5. *Student Profile*—where students could create Web sites

(continued)

(continued)

This set of five areas excluded the majority of default features available in the CMS. As the project's manager and educational designer, I decided to make the Web site template simple, containing only those tools I believed would be of immediate use.

Challenges

- Content is usually tied to a course. This means that often what a student contributes to one course Web site, for example postings to a forum, is not accessible from others. Neither is the content easily transferred between sites. Another result of content being tied to a course is that when a course finishes, a student's contributions are no longer accessible. These problems occur because many CMSs are structured on a course-by-course model, rather than a student-centered model.
- Access can be difficult if the system does not accept the student's username, password, or both. This is not always the fault of the CMS. Often institutions do not have adequate procedures in place to ensure that students' enrollment details are entered into the system and to ensure students are made aware of their usernames and passwords.
- The common navigation method, and other design similarities, can make visiting course Web sites a sterile and repetitive task.
- Institutions, including teachers, may consider a CMS as the solution to their need to be seen as using the Internet. A CMS is not a solution. Instead, it is a start that, without the commitment of an institution's staff, will result in students being disappointed. Often institutions say they have hundreds of courses online. Yet in reality the hundreds of sites are equivalent to having lots of television channels showing nothing but a test pattern.
- The structure and language used in a CMS reflect that of the culture in which the developers live. For example, the word *course* means different things in different countries. Although changing the CMS structure and language is possible, the process is not intuitive and the default settings are often used.

Teachers' Perspectives

The advantages and disadvantages from the teacher's perspective should also be considered.

Advantages

- A CMS is a quick and relatively painless way of starting to use the Internet as a teaching resource.
- A CMS can help teachers concentrate on how to use the Internet to help students, rather than having to concentrate on the technical and design aspects of developing and maintaining Web sites.
- The structure of many CMSs is based on the curriculum structure commonly used in on-campus courses. We all feel most comfortable in familiar surroundings. This familiarity can encourage and help teachers use the Internet as a teaching and learning resource.
- A CMS can be adapted to meet the varying needs and skills of teachers. For example, some teachers may want to use a synchronous chat tool, while their colleagues prefer that the tool is not part of their Web sites.
- The student management features, such as the ability to track attempts at quizzes and Web pages visited, are useful.

Challenges

- So many tools and features can be included in a Web site that it can be overwhelming. It is best to start with a few and add more as teachers and students become familiar with the system.
- A CMS can limit what teachers use course Web sites for and suppress their creativity. Although CMSs offer many options, they do imply that there is one ideal way of structuring a Web site.
- The many things that can be recorded, such as students' quiz attempts, pages visited, and time spent on each page, can result in a focus on the numbers for evidence of success, rather than investigating the extent to which the students have been helped in developing their understandings of course content.
- Placing material on CMS Web sites is not as intuitive and easy, for most teachers, as is commonly advertised by CMS vendors.

- Institutional managers can see a CMS as the answer, the magic solution, to their desire to be seen as an Internet-embracing organization. This unrealistic expectation negatively affects teachers.

We Must Have a Course Management System; Our Competitors Do!

A challenge when deciding whether to use a CMS is to base any decision on the needs and wants of students first, teachers second, and then the institution. Unfortunately, this order is often reversed. My advice to teachers is as follows:

- Remember that CMS vendors measure success on the basis of the number of licenses they sell. You measure success differently.
- You may not need to use a CMS. Such systems are one of many teaching and learning tools. Recommendations about whether teachers should use a CMS are in Topic 9.3.
- You do not need to purchase a particular system because your competitors have. The advantages to a CMS vendor of having

many institutions in the same geographical area using the same system are significant. They may not be significant for your institution (see Exhibit 9.2).

CMSs also have advantages and challenges from an institutional standpoint.

Advantage

- Purchasing a CMS is a quick way of establishing a computer system designed to support Internet-based teaching and learning.

Challenges

- Installing a CMS is only the start of the process of using the Internet to help teachers teach and students learn. There is a danger that the focus will be on the technical rather than the educational infrastructure.
- Choosing which CMS to use is a significant decision as once a system is installed, it is difficult to change. Due to the lack of standards in the underlying code of CMSs, transferring content between them is problematic.

Should We Develop or Buy a Course Management System?

Creating a CMS means that a system specifically designed to meet the needs and wants of the institution's teachers and students can be developed. However, in most contexts it is better to buy a system. Why? My reasons relate to the many challenges associated with creating a system. These include

- the need for a skillful team of computer programmers, to be employed for years;
- the need for the development team, including educational designers, teachers, and students, to be involved for many years as the system is gradually developed; and therefore
- the large financial costs.

EXHIBIT 9.2. The Challenges of Implementing
a Course Management System

In Topic 9.1, the features of Web sites developed in a hotel and tourism management school are described. I was the school's project manager and educational designer. Not all of the following difficulties are applicable to every CMS implementation. My aim is to list them so that you can be aware of and plan accordingly for likely challenges.

The school was one of the first to develop course Web sites using the CMS recently purchased by the institution. Therefore, the school and the institution's computer specialists learned a lot during the first two semesters. As our experiences increased, procedures to minimize the following challenges were developed:

- *Access difficulties:* Many students' usernames and passwords, required to access the CMS, did not immediately work. During the first four weeks of a semester, the majority of an assistant's time was devoted to solving this problem. The main reasons for access denials were imperfect coordination between the enrollment office and those responsible for uploading student details, and the case-sensitive nature of the usernames and passwords.
- *Multistep procedures for placing materials on a Web site:* The procedures for converting files, such as lecture slides and handouts, to a Web format involved many steps. Although teachers received handouts describing the steps and practiced them during training sessions, many became frustrated and reluctant to place their materials online.
- *The need to understand the file structure of the CMS:* Not every teacher understood how to interact with the CMS Web server, how to upload files into particular server locations, how file names were case sensitive, and the need to update the students' view, different from the teacher's view, once files were in the server. By themselves each of these points is small and solvable. However, the more hurdles teachers faced in using the system, the more reluctant they were to use it.
- *New versions of the CMS:* The process of learning how to interact with the CMS was never ending. Just as everyone became familiar with one version, a new one would be installed that added features and required small changes in procedures for placing material on Web sites. System updates are to be expected and welcomed. However, more than one update each year tests the willingness of teachers and students to learn new tools and methods.

If your institution has sufficient funds to employ an experienced team of programmers and educational designers, devoted to one project, it is rewarding to create a system.

If a CMS is to be purchased, the decision about which one to buy is made at the institutional or school level. An advantage of an institution-wide system is that the infrastructure necessary to maintain it is paid for at the institutional level. Also, economies of scale can play a part in negotiating the site license and support agreement with the vendor.

The following points are worth keeping in mind when deciding which CMS to buy:

- To what extent will the system meet the needs and wants of teachers and students? Collis and Moonen (2001) provide information useful to people seeking an answer to this question. Their discussion focuses on the educational aspects, independent of specific commercial systems.
- What is the support infrastructure—both educational and technical—that is required? What support will the vendor provide? Training and support issues are discussed in Topic 9.4.
- To what extent does the CMS integrate with systems already in use? For example, how difficult is it to transfer content between systems? To what extent can the proposed CMS be integrated with the institution's enrollment and administration system?
- What are the ongoing license fees?
- To what extent is the underlying code locked? Locked code will inhibit modification of the CMS design and functionality to better meet the institution's teaching and learning environment.
- Try before you buy. Establish a pilot group of teachers, students, educational designers, and computer programmers to try out the CMS.

TOPIC 9.3: A TEACHER'S PERSPECTIVE—
USING A COURSE MANAGEMENT SYSTEM

This topic is addressed to teachers. If you want to provide Internet-based learning opportunities, for example, a course Web site (Chapter 7) and communication tools (Chapter 8), you do not have to use a CMS. You must consider the following factors before committing to using a CMS:

- Consider the needs, wants, and technology of the students.
- Do you want total control over the design of your Web site or are you prepared to use a template? Although you can still be creative, a CMS does limit your choices.
- If you want to learn about the foundations of Web design and development, do not use a CMS. The reason is that a CMS is designed for teachers who, for whatever reason, prefer to use a template and be provided with routines to establish and maintain a Web site.

- Ask about the types of support, both technical and educational, which the institution provides. A CMS has to be maintained by computer specialists. It is of little use having a system if you do not know how best to use it to help students.
- How much practice has your institution had at maintaining a CMS? For example, ensuring that students have access to course sites they are enrolled in is a challenge. It involves coordination between the information technology office and the enrollment office. When an institution is using a CMS for the first time, expect confusion and frustration.
- There is little point in having a course Web site unless you are prepared to use it throughout the semester and thereby encourage students to value it. A successful course Web site involves you doing more than posting copies of the lecture notes.
- Remember that you are the best judge of whether a CMS Web site will benefit you and your students. Treat the words of CMS vendors with skepticism. Knowing that many prestigious universities use a particular CMS tells you little about the extent to which it may benefit your students. Knowing that there have been thousands of visits to the Web sites your colleagues have created tells you little about what students did while visiting the pages and the extent to which the sites helped them.

There is a tendency to think of CMSs only being used in flexible learning environments, where students infrequently, if ever, attend on-campus, face-to-face classes. However, such systems can also be of use to students who attend weekly on-campus lectures and tutorials. This was the situation I described in Topic 9.1 and Williams (2003), where the CMS Web sites were used as supplementary resources, supporting the core resources of the face-to-face lectures and tutorials. Students were asked how they would like teachers to use the Web sites. Their responses were summarized, resulting in the following ten guidelines:

1. Post information about journal articles and supplementary readings related to concepts discussed in lectures and tutorials.
2. Make past exam papers available, with incomplete answers.

3. Post information about the industry that relates to recently discussed course concepts.
4. Recommend Web sites, including reasons why students should visit them.
5. Create self-assessment quizzes. Although the quiz types in CMSs are simplistic, students appreciate them.
6. If you plan to use synchronous communication tools, such as chat, make sure you set the consultation hours when you will be online.
7. Encourage students to communicate with you and their fellow students through asynchronous communication environments, such as a Web forum, a Listserv, and e-mail.
8. Use a CMS calendar tool as a teacher-to-student diary.
9. Have a part of the Web site devoted to information about employment opportunities.
10. After your lecture, place any electronic notes you used on the Web site.

Beware of Numbers

Course management systems are good at collecting and summarizing data about every visit to every page in a Web site. However, you need to look behind the numbers and use the data as only one of many sources of information about Web site effectiveness. As described in Williams (2003):

> 2,000 hits to a page in a Web site sounds impressive. However, what does the number mean if the page is empty? Are students lost? Are they just checking? And if the page does contain information to what extent was it useful? And why do some students visit the page for five seconds, and others for 30 minutes? Are they really spending 30 minutes considering the information, or talking to a friend or getting a cup of coffee? (p. 63)

TOPIC 9.4: TRAINING AND SUPPORT ROLES

This topic is addressed to project managers, educational designers, and teachers. To help teachers and students use a CMS, a training and support structure, focusing on computer literacy and educational is-

sues, is required. The educational aspects are often neglected. As Collis and Moonen (2001) stated in relation to staff development, "Many times the focus is directly on the technology itself rather than on the pedagogy and strategy of managing the technology in instruction" (p. 63). An educational designer will find the following guidelines useful when helping teachers use a CMS.

Training and Support Guidelines

A teacher using a CMS will find the following guidelines useful.

Technical Issues

- Remember that learning how to use a CMS is not easy and intuitive for everyone.
- Realize that not all teachers want to learn, or have the time required to learn, how to maintain a Web site.

- Make sure that people involved in helping teachers learn about a CMS understand the needs and wants of teachers. A common mistake is to have a training session presented by computer specialists who have little understanding of the audience's level of computer literacy.
- Hold training sessions in front of computers at least a month before the semester. Teachers need time to learn, experiment, and construct their course Web sites. Ensure that supporting paper documentation is distributed.
- Tell teachers about the tutorials and instant help that are available in a CMS.
- Designate a person to be available throughout the semester to support teachers with the creation and maintenance of course Web sites.

Educational Issues

- Make teachers aware of the successes and failures that their colleagues have had with CMSs.
- Teachers listen to and respect students' opinions. Therefore, base recommendations about the types of activities to use with a CMS on what students say they need and want.
- Have an educational designer available throughout the semester to support teachers in considering how to use a CMS to help students understand their courses.

Not Every Teacher Wants to Be, or Can Be, a Web Site Designer, Developer, and Maintenance Expert

There is a tendency for vendors and institutions to promote a CMS as a tool that teachers can use by themselves. For some teachers this is true. For the majority it is not. Instead, teachers want to work with others to create and maintain their course Web sites.

The creation and maintenance of a CMS Web site is not an intuitive process. Plus, many teachers do not have the time or desire to learn the required skills. A teacher's main role is to help students develop their understandings of course content. It is not to help students with their CMS access problems or to spend hours learning how to upload materials. It is the responsibility of an institution to ensure that a support structure is in place to allow teachers to focus on their main role.

Therefore, I advocate employing specific people to help teachers with both the technical and educational aspects of using a CMS. For example, a person should be employed to help teachers learn how to upload files into the system, and to do the uploading for teachers when necessary.

I recognize that some teachers do not need help in creating and maintaining Web sites. My concern is that senior management of an institution, through the influence of CMS vendors, can incorrectly assume that all teachers have the time, ability, and desire to fill the many roles associated with a successful Web site. This assumption is invalid and is detrimental to teachers and students, and in the long term detrimental to the institution.

Providing a Training and Support Infrastructure for Students

Teachers, project managers, and educational designers helping students use a CMS will find the following guidelines helpful.

Technical Issues

- Do not assume learning how to use a CMS is easy. Not all students are computer experts.
- In the first weeks of the semester, hold training sessions in front of computers for students.
- Tell students about the tutorials and instant help that are available in a CMS.
- Make sure students know where they can go to solve their technical problems. For example, there will be students whose usernames and passwords do not work. Have a procedure, developed before the semester starts, to solve such problems.

Educational Issues

- Arrange for teachers to explain to students, in the first weeks of the semester, how the CMS can help students learn and what role the teacher will play.
- Advertise the CMS. Students need to be made aware of the system. The advertising plan involves teachers explaining the sys-

tem, and advertisements on notice boards explaining the main features of a course Web site and how to access it.
- Ensure students are aware of the support services available.

KEY POINTS

1. As a teacher, resist the pressure to have a course Web site, delivered through a CMS, until you are convinced of the benefits to students and your commitment to developing and maintaining it.
2. Make the decision about which CMS to buy after considering first, the educational needs and wants of students, second, the needs and wants of teachers, third, technical implementation issues, and fourth, the actions of competing institutions.

Chapter 10

Teaching in a Flexible Learning Environment

Once learning resources have been developed, consideration should be given to how best to integrate them into the teaching and learning environment. Otherwise they will be left on teachers' office shelves.

A teacher undertakes many activities before and during a flexible learning course. As in all teaching, communication is a key component of helping students. In a flexible learning course, activities such as on-campus classes and regular e-mails are important in ensuring students are not isolated.

OBJECTIVES

1. To emphasize that to ensure that developed resources are used, it is necessary to give deliberate consideration to how best to integrate them into a flexible learning environment
2. To describe the actions of a teacher before a course starts
3. To list the types of information a teacher emphasizes at the start of a course
4. To provide recommendations about the actions of a teacher during a course, and, in particular, to recommend the distribution of a weekly e-mail and group-based activities in on-campus classes
5. To describe how an educational designer, acting as a staff development officer, can assist a teacher during a course

TOPIC 10.1: INTRODUCTION

The majority of this chapter is particularly relevant to teachers, as it is about teaching in a flexible learning environment. Topic 10.5 is the one topic addressed to educational designers. It describes how they can assist teachers.

Although the emphasis in Chapters 4 to 9 was on developing flexible learning resources, Chapters 10 and 11 are about ensuring that these resources are integrated into teaching and learning environments. I have read about and been involved in too many projects for which quality resources are developed but not used. Instead they sit on teachers' shelves gathering dust. The following are the characteristics of this chapter:

- The role of teachers is emphasized. The advice is targeted at teachers new to flexible learning.
- The information is independent of the types of learning resources used. That is, the focus is on the general teaching and

learning environment rather than the specific combination of print-based packages, Web sites, videos, and so on.
- The advice applies to flexible learning environments in which students have some control over which learning resources they use, and when and how they use them.
- Although the term *semester* is used, the information is relevant not only in institutions that have such a structure. In this handbook, *semester* implies any period of time in which students start and complete the study of a course.

TOPIC 10.2: BEFORE A COURSE STARTS

The following are activities a teacher should undertake before a course starts:

- *Become familiar with the structure and content of the learning resources.* Often you will use resources that were developed by other teachers. In such situations, you need to become familiar with the structure and content of the resources. In particular, given the wide range in Web site designs, it is worthwhile spending time navigating a course site and in the process becoming familiar with how the site helps students answer the questions: Where am I? Where can I go? What have I seen?
- *Become technically proficient in using the resources.* For example, if a course Web site or a CD-ROM simulation requires the installation of plug-in software, you need to know how to install it. Although you can refer complex technical issues to support staff, you should be able to help students with usability issues.
- *Develop an understanding of the flexible learning process.* If you have not taught in the institution's flexible learning program before:
  a. ask fellow teachers to tell you about their good and bad experiences;
  b. discuss the teaching process with an educational designer; and
  c. consult books, journals, and Web sites about teaching in such environments.
- *Coordinate with other courses.* Students are most likely to be studying more than one course. By discussing the program of

study with other teachers, you can help maximize the benefits of flexible learning for students.

a. Assignment submission dates can be arranged so that students do not have to submit all assignments in the same week.

b. Any on-campus classes can be held on the same day to help students make the most of their campus visits. It is a feature of many flexible learning environments that students decide whether they attend on-campus classes. To have classes distributed throughout a week reduces this flexibility. For example, for two courses, each with weekly optional-attendance classes, the timetable should be organized so that they are on the same day.

- *Be involved with orientation activities.* If orientation activities are held, make sure you are involved in their planning and implementation. The more you are involved, the greater your understanding of the challenges that students face and the quicker you will become known to students.

Orientation Activities for First-Year Students

In the first semester of a flexible learning program, first-year students usually complete orientation activities, which are designed to help them develop an awareness of their roles, the roles of teachers, and the supporting infrastructure. Orientation activities focus on describing the general teaching and learning environment. Specific details about each course are provided during the first week of the semester.

Ideally, the activities are part of a face-to-face orientation day held just before the semester starts (see Exhibit 10.1). However, this is not always possible due to factors such as students' work commitments. It may be inconvenient for them to come to the institution. In such situations, the activities need to be sent to students. For example, a video can be developed that introduces the institution, the program of study, and the teachers and explains the methods of communication. The following types of information should be included in orientation activities:

- An introduction to the institution
- An introduction to the teachers

- An overview of the program of study that emphasizes the requirements for successful completion of courses
- Learning and study skills associated with being a successful flexible learning student
- The communication channels between students and teachers, and, in particular, demonstration of any computer-mediated contact environments, such as Web forums
- The support resources available, for example, information about the school's administration office that can help with enrollments and assignment submission procedures, as well as the services offered by the institution's student services office
- Descriptions of learning resources useful in all courses, such as an institution's library services

TOPIC 10.3: THE START OF A COURSE

During the first few weeks, it is important that the teacher emphasizes particular aspects of the course and the flexible learning process (see Exhibit 10.2). Students need to be made aware of the teacher's expectations and what they can expect from the teacher. The following information should be emphasized by a teacher at the start of a course:

EXHIBIT 10.1. The Orientation Days

For the courses in the HTM Project, all first-year students lived in Hong Kong. Therefore they could attend a compulsory orientation day held a week before the start of the first semester. Because the students came to the campus, we were able to design activities to encourage a sense of community, as well as to convey information such as that described in Topic 10.2.

Activities to encourage a sense of community included introductory talks by the teachers and the opportunity to meet them at morning tea. Also group activities to help students get to know their colleagues were held. Significant time was devoted to encouraging students to build informal support networks. Another activity involved second-year students describing their flexible learning experiences.

EXHIBIT 10.2. The Week 1 Compulsory Class

For each of the ten courses in the HTM Project, it was compulsory for students to attend a three-hour class in the first week. For example, students who studied two courses per semester attended six hours on the same day in week 1 of the fourteen-week semester.

Although each teacher decided the format of the compulsory class, the following were the main events:

- Each student signed a class list and received the print-based course package.
- The amount of emphasis placed on the following aspects of the course depended on whether students had studied flexible learning courses in previous semesters: the suggested study schedule, the ways of contacting the teacher and other students, and the assignment submission procedures.
- The on-campus attendance scheme involved four strongly encouraged three-hour classes in weeks 4, 8, 12, and 13, and optional-attendance two-hour consultation sessions in the other weeks. In the first week the teacher explained what would be done in the three-hour classes and how they would be different from the consultation sessions.
- For first-year students, there were activities designed to encourage them to get to know their fellow students and start to form support networks.
- At least the final hour of the class was devoted to the students starting the package. Usually the teacher would present a summary of the first unit, and then in small groups students would attempt the self-exercises.

- *The importance of the course outline:* Emphasis should be placed on the important parts of the outline, such as the suggested study schedule, the communication channels, and assignment submission procedures.
- *The importance of maintaining a regular study schedule.*
- *How to technically and educationally use the learning resources:* For example, if you have a course Web site, provide instructions about any usernames and passwords, how to install any required software, how to navigate the site, and ways in which it can help students understand course concepts.
- *The types of communication channels and their importance:* You need to describe the communication channels available and

use them to contact students. Be proactive. Do not wait for students to contact you, as they may incorrectly believe that in a flexible learning environment they are not meant to contact the teacher.

- *The speed at which you will reply to e-mails:* Some teachers place unnecessary pressure on themselves by not explicitly telling students how soon they will reply to e-mails. If students are not told, many will expect a rapid reply. Tell students that you will aim to reply to an e-mail within a specific number of days of receiving it.

- *Explanations of what you will do in any on-campus classes:* Some flexible learning environments have on-campus classes that students can choose to attend. Once you have described your plans for such classes, students can make informed decisions about whether to attend. For example, you may say that such classes will concentrate on providing group activities best done face-to-face.

- *The need to start studying the course content as soon as possible:* Emphasize that every week that passes is one less week before the end of the course. Make it obvious to students that they should make a start on their studies. For example, if you have an on-campus class, start reviewing the content. Or send an e-mail at the end of the first week stating that students should have made a start and include some questions that they will be able to answer if they have started their studies.

TOPIC 10.4: DURING A COURSE

This topic focuses on the teacher's roles once a course has started. Many teachers have an uncomfortable feeling during a flexible learning course. It is a feeling of uncertainty, of unease, at not regularly seeing students. Such feelings lessen as the teacher is involved in more courses and sees that students successfully complete them. A key point is that flexible learning does not have to mean less communication with students compared to compulsory weekly on-campus courses. In fact, it can mean more and better quality communication. As emphasized throughout this handbook, flexible learning is not about reducing teachers' roles. On the contrary, a teacher can take advantage of numerous methods to maximize the course potential:

- *Send a weekly e-mail.* A weekly e-mail can help keep students on task by reminding them of the sections of the resources they should be studying, testing their understandings of sections, and reminding them that they can contact you.
- *Regularly remind students of ways in which they can communicate with you and their fellow students.*
- *Make the most of any on-campus classes.* If the course contains on-campus classes, use most of the time on activities that are best done in a face-to-face environment, such as group role-playing scenarios and activities that are logistically easier on campus.
- *Maintain a diary of student contact.* Keep a record of contacts you have with students. You do this for a number of reasons:
  a. By reviewing the diary, you can decide whether you need to contact students who are late submitting assignments.
  b. Regularly reviewing the diary can help reassure you that students are studying and help allay any concerns about not seeing the students every week.
  c. The diary is a source of information about the efforts of students and yourself. At the end of semester when you are deciding the students' grades, a record of their contacts provides some evidence of their efforts. If students appeal their grades, the diary can support your decisions.
- *Tell students when you are away from your office.* If you are going to be away for a few days, for example at a conference, tell students. If you are not going to be accessible by e-mail, set up your mail software so that it automatically acknowledges received e-mails and states when you will return.

The Weekly E-Mail

The content of a weekly e-mail is dependent on whether a course also uses an asynchronous group communication tool, such as a Web forum (Chapter 8). If so, then some of what is contained in a weekly e-mail can instead be posted to the forum. Regardless of the other computer-mediated contact tools used, I recommend that a weekly course e-mail be distributed. Such an e-mail should

- be short with the most important information at the top;
- contain clear headings to help students scan for useful information;
- be sent at approximately the same time each week so that students know when to expect it;
- contain the teacher's contact details; and
- be sent using a suppressed list of recipients so that the students' addresses are not shown.

Figure 10.1 illustrates the type of content to include in a weekly e-mail. The main purposes of such e-mails are to keep students motivated and studying by reminding them of the sections of the core resources they should be studying, testing their understandings of past sections, and reminding them of how they can contact the teacher and fellow students.

On-Campus Classes

A flexible learning course may have some on-campus classes, which can be a combination of compulsory attendance and optional-attendance classes. For example, in a fourteen-week semester, attendance in week 1 can be compulsory, with voluntary attendance classes in weeks 4, 8, and 12. On-campus classes are an ideal time for

---

From: Ms. Berg [Teacher]
Date: Monday, 6 October 2003 10:00 AM
To: Strategic Management Students [Semester 1 03/04]
Subject: Week 5 E-Mail–Strategic Management

Welcome to the Week 5 E-Mail.

*** **Important Notes** ***
Remember that by the end of week 6 your first assignment has to be submitted.

In week 8 there is an on-campus class you are strongly encouraged to attend. A video about recent trends in strategic management will be shown.

*** **What you should be studying** ***
This week you should be starting Unit 5: The Environment.

One part of the unit—Porter's Five Forces—can be difficult to understand. Make sure you can complete self-exercise 3.

*** **Review of Unit 3** ***
By now you should have completed Unit 3: Vision, Mission, and Objectives.

Some Quiz Questions:
1. Draw a diagram showing the relationships of vision, mission, and objectives to corporate, business, and functional-level strategies.
2. For a local restaurant list the possible types of stakeholders.
3. In what ways are business unit objectives different from corporate-level objectives?

*** **Contact** ***
The Web forum is working well and lots of you are posting messages. Thanks! I have just posted two more debate points you can respond to.

I try my best to reply to e-mails within 48 hours, so do not hesitate to contact me.

Regards,
Ms. Berg
Phone: 5421 1245
E-mail: iberg@institution.edu
Office 815, Building 5

FIGURE 10.1. A Weekly E-Mail Sent by the Teacher of a Strategic Management Course

learning activities that are best completed in a face-to-face environment or are logistically easier to offer when students are together. If attendance at on-campus classes is optional, the teacher needs to convince students of the benefits of attending. The activities need to be qualitatively different from those included in the resources students can use off campus. The following are some of the types of activities that can be provided:

- *A review of course content:* The teacher can review the most recent course content, which should have been studied since the last on-campus class. Such a review can help students identify the parts of the course the teacher considers most important, or challenging, or both. It will help students who have studied the material to reflect on their understandings while motivating those who are falling behind the suggested study schedule.
- *Group activities:* On-campus classes provide the ideal environment for group face-to-face activities. In such environments, students can interact and learn in ways qualitatively different than those possible when only communicating through computer-mediated contact tools.
- *A question-and-answer session:* A part of an on-campus class can be devoted to students asking questions related to the course content and structure. Sometimes students can be reluctant to ask questions directly of the teacher. In such situations, a useful technique is to form small groups of students and ask them to write down three questions about parts of the course they are unsure of. The teacher collects the questions and uses them to guide the question-and-answer session.
- *Activities logistically suited to on-campus classes:* Some activities have to be completed on-campus due to the specialized equipment required. For example, many science courses require laboratory sessions. Other activities are logistically easier to conduct when students are all together. For example, in a services management course, a teacher may want students to watch a video of interviews with hotel managers about the essential components of quality service. Such a video could be duplicated, in accordance with the copyright license, and posted to each student. Alternatively, showing the video in an on-campus class can save the time and costs of such a process.

TOPIC 10.5: THE RESPONSIBILITIES
OF EDUCATIONAL DESIGNERS

Teachers should be able to call upon the support of educational designers (see Exhibit 10.3). This is particularly the case when teachers are experiencing a flexible learning environment for the first time. In this situation, an educational designer acts as a staff development officer helping teachers apply the strategies discussed in the preceding Chapter 10 topics. The following recommendations are for educational designers assisting teachers in a flexible learning environment:

- *Be familiar with what a teacher needs to do before, at the start, and during a course.*
- *Ensure that every teacher knows the other teachers involved in a flexible learning program of study.* Do not assume that a person is aware of who else is teaching flexible learning courses. Organize meetings during which experiences can be shared and difficulties resolved.
- *Each teacher is different and will need and want different types of support.* Efforts to help teachers should be based on an understanding of their prior experiences. Use a combination of techniques such as one-on-one meetings and group seminars.
- *Be proactive and offer assistance.* Many teachers are willing to approach an educational designer for advice. However, some are not. You need to be proactive without being forceful and appearing to tell teachers what to do.
- *Make sure that teachers receive copies of the learning resources well in advance of courses starting.*
- *Keep a diary summarizing your discussions with teachers.* The ideas and experiences of teachers can improve the design of resources and the structure of curricula.
- *Ask if you can be an observer in on-campus classes and computer-mediated contact environments.* If the teacher and students agree, such observations can help you alter the design of flexible learning environments to better meet the needs and wants of students and teachers.

EXHIBIT 10.3. The Support of an Educational Designer

As an educational designer in the HTM Project, I tried to assist teachers by the following actions:

- A month before a semester started, I met with each teacher for a general discussion about the flexible learning environment.
- A week before the semester, I sent teachers an e-mail containing recommendations about the week 1 compulsory class.
- A week before the first on-campus class students were strongly encouraged to attend, I sent an e-mail about the types of activities teachers could include.

The amount and type of contact with teachers depended on their experiences and willingness to talk. There was a lot of informal contact. An educational designer needs to achieve a balance between being seen as someone who can help and being perceived as someone who is interfering. A benefit of having my office in the school was that it was easier for teachers to approach me and to have informal discussions, for example during a staff tea break. My aim was not only to assist them, but to also obtain their advice about how the flexible learning environment could be improved.

KEY POINTS

1. As a teacher, be involved in the planning and running of orientation-day activities for first-year students.
2. As a teacher, consider sending a weekly e-mail to help students keep on task and self-evaluate their understandings. Such e-mails also assure students that you care and are available to help.
3. On-campus classes that students can choose to attend should contain activities that enhance the resources students use off campus and offer opportunities to interact face-to-face with teachers and fellow students.

Chapter 11

Being a Student in a Flexible Learning Environment

For a student, a flexible learning environment can be challenging. Not only do students have expectations of their teachers, the teachers also have expectations of the students.

Students need to continually question themselves about why they are using particular learning resources and whether they understand the course content. On-campus classes and Internet-based discussion forums are important in promoting contact between teachers and students. Such communication is as important in flexible learning as it is in on-campus courses.

OBJECTIVES

1. To describe the advantages and challenges for students of a flexible learning environment
2. To list questions for students to ask themselves at the start and during a flexible learning course
3. To emphasize that maintaining a flexible learning environment is a team effort and that just as a teacher has expectations of students, they have expectations of the teacher
4. To provide strategies students can apply when using print-based course packages and course Web sites

This chapter directly addresses students who are studying courses in a flexible learning environment. Therefore, teachers and educational designers will need to imagine that they are students. No assumptions are made that previous chapters in this handbook have been read. The chapter is written this way to facilitate its sharing with students.

TOPIC 11.1: INTRODUCTION

The objective of this chapter is to help you, the student, be successful when studying flexible learning courses. Such environments offer advantages and challenges different from those you may have experienced before. In such an environment, you have some control over which learning resources you use, when you use them, and how you use them. Some courses include both compulsory and optional on-campus classes. However, in many courses you do not attend the physical, that is, "bricks-and-mortar," campus at all.

Learning resources are things you use to develop an understanding of course content. They are sources of information. Examples are

teachers, fellow students, work colleagues, libraries, Web sites, paper notes, CD-ROMs, videos, television programs, newspapers, and text-books.

You may be an undergraduate student and may have heard that flexible learning is only for postgraduates. This is not true. You do not have to be a certain age to be a successful student. What is important is that you have the motivation to learn and are committed and disci-plined. You may have heard that certain study skills are required. This is true. It is great if you already have the skills. However, most stu-dents develop and refine them as they are studying.

A flexible learning environment is not totally different from that of on-campus courses. Think of it like this. Learning is a sport. On-cam-pus courses and flexible learning courses are variations of the same sport. So although you do need some extra flexible learning skills, you also need to apply the ones you already have. For example, if someone thinks they can be successful by only reading the course notes the week before the exam, then their chances of passing are small, regardless of whether it is an on-campus course with weekly lectures and tutorials or a flexible learning course. The rest of this chapter aims to help you prepare for a flexible learning environment:

- Topic 11.2 considers the advantages and challenges.
- Topic 11.3 lists questions to ask at the start of a course and as the weeks pass.
- Topic 11.4 is about strategies for using print-based packages and course Web sites.

TOPIC 11.2: THE ADVANTAGES AND CHALLENGES OF FLEXIBLE LEARNING

Flexible learning can be liberating. You can feel free and able to make decisions. It can also be scary! You may be uncertain about how you will cope. I have asked many students to describe the good and the bad of flexible learning. In this topic, their thoughts are summa-rized.

Advantages

In a flexible learning environment, you have increased responsibility for your learning decisions compared to courses where weekly on-campus lecture and tutorial attendance is compulsory. As you consider the following list of the potential advantages, keep in mind that the types and amount of flexibility depend on the course, the teacher, and the institution. For example, one course may stipulate four compulsory classes and optional attendance in other weeks. A similar course offered by another institution may involve no on-campus classes.

- You may have a degree of control over on-campus attendance. For example, a course may involve no on-campus classes or some combination of compulsory and optional classes.

- You may have some control over the pace of learning. For example, a course can have a suggested study schedule, but the actual speed at which you study is your decision.
- You may have choices in regard to the types of communication with a teacher and the frequency of contact. For example, a teacher can offer a variety of contact methods, such as e-mail, phone, and visiting the teacher's office, and you decide which ones to use and when you want to make contact.
- You may have choices about the types and frequency of contact with other students. For example, a course may have an Internet-based Web forum and an assessment scheme that requires you to contribute to forum debates. Another course may include a Web forum but make contributing messages voluntary.
- Some courses have a degree of student control over the syllabus. For example, in many postgraduate courses the learning objectives are broad, and you choose, with guidance from teachers, the specific topics that you plan to learn about.
- You may have a degree of control over whether to study particular course content. That is, you decide whether you already understand a topic and therefore do not need to study the notes. For example, some learning resources include self-exercises you try before studying the notes. By comparing your attempts to the provided solutions, you self-assess whether you need to read the course notes.
- You may have some control over the sequence of course content. For example, a learning package containing twelve units of material may have an implied sequence from unit 1 to unit 12. However, you are able to vary that sequence.
- You may have some choice over the learning resources you use to understand course content. For example, you know that your understanding of a particular topic needs to be improved. So you decide to study the course notes written by the teacher and read the recommended journal articles. You also decide to search for some Web sites about the topic and look for related articles in newspapers.
- Some courses include a degree of student control over the assessment structure. This involves choosing the types and number of assessment activities.

Challenges

A flexible learning environment can be challenging and you may be worried about whether you will cope. Some of the following common concerns may apply to you. Often, realizing that you are not the only person with a particular concern is the first step to overcoming it. Applying the strategies in Topics 11.3 and 11.4 will alleviate many of these concerns.

I Lack Self-Discipline and Need to Be Told
What, Where, and When to Study

You have to be self-disciplined to be successful in a flexible learning course. Unfortunately for many people, when they have control over their study schedule the world becomes an even more fascinating place and they want to explore it, instead of sitting down and studying. It is important to make a good start in a course. So do not hesitate to seek the advice of the teacher and the institution's support services.

I Will Not Be Able to Keep to the Study Schedule

Most flexible learning courses have a suggested study schedule. It is important to remember that such a schedule is designed to help you plan. It is not compulsory. After all, a major advantage of flexible learning is that you can coordinate study with professional and personal responsibilities. For example, work may involve traveling overseas, and finding time to study the course notes can be difficult. In such a situation, you aim to put in more study hours when you return home. We all learn in different ways. Some of us aim to study a little every day. Others study intensely for one day of the week. It is your choice.

How Will I Be Successful When I Do Not See the Teacher
Every Week?

There are three points to think about. First, you should not need to see the teacher every week because the learning resources, such as course notes and Web sites, are designed to support self-study. Second, flexible learning does not mean zero communication with the teacher. In fact, you should make regular contact. Third, seeing a teacher does not necessarily mean better learning. Think about the courses you have studied that involved seeing teachers regularly. Did you make contact during the classes? Did you communicate with them by asking questions? Or did you sit in lecture halls listening and writing notes? I am not saying that lectures are bad, but I am saying that face-to-face contact is not a prerequisite for learning.

The Course Includes On-Campus Classes and I Will Not Be Able to Attend

Although many courses have no on-campus classes, some do have a combination of compulsory and optional classes. These can take the form of residential camps in which you come to the campus for two or more consecutive days. Before enrolling in a course, ensure that you will be able to attend any compulsory classes. If you unexpectedly find yourself unable to attend, contact the teacher as soon as possible. If a course has on-campus classes that are optional, then not being able to attend is not such a problem. What it does mean is that you need to ensure that you communicate with the teacher through other means, such as the phone and e-mail. Also, try to be part of a student group that meets regularly either face-to-face or on the Internet.

Why Am I Paying More Than Students Who Complete a Similar Course with On-Campus Lectures and Tutorials?

Many institutions charge higher fees for flexible learning courses than for equivalent fully on-campus courses. Why? One reason is that flexible learning courses are a good source of revenue. An institution will charge a fee that will maximize its profit while ensuring full enrollment. It is a demand versus supply situation. In addition, the supply of quality flexible learning courses is less than the demand.

In a course you should receive learning resources, such as packages and course Web sites, which are produced to a high educational standard. Often these resources are not provided to students attending weekly on-campus lectures and tutorials. In addition to self-study resources, the course should offer many ways of communicating with the teacher and other students. In fact, the range of learning resources, including opportunities to interact with the teacher and other students, can be far greater in a flexible environment than in an on-campus situation.

TOPIC 11.3: YOU HAVE ENROLLED IN A FLEXIBLE LEARNING COURSE—WHAT NOW?

The first part of this topic lists questions to ask yourself at the start of a course and during a course. These can help you make the most of

the opportunities a flexible learning environment offers while minimizing the challenges. Next is a discussion about what you can expect of the teacher and what the teacher can expect from you. The topic concludes with recommendations about maximizing the benefits of any on-campus classes.

The Start of a Course

To help establish a good foundation for a course, ask yourself the following questions:

- Have I read and understood the course outline document, which contains important dates and information about using the learning resources and completing assignments?
- Do I have copies of, or access to, all essential resources?
- Have I designed a study schedule that includes important dates, such as
  a. when assignments are due;
  b. examination dates;
  c. the days and times of any Internet-based discussions; and
  d. the days and times of any on-campus classes I want to attend?
- Do I know the teacher's e-mail address and phone number?
- Have I sent an e-mail to the teacher introducing myself?
- What are the ways in which I can publicly and privately discuss the course with fellow students?
- Are there other students who either work or live near me so that we can form a support network that meets face-to-face?
- Have I checked that I can access and post messages to Internet discussion forums?
- If I need some extra learning resources, how can I get them? For example, I may need to get some journal articles. Can I ask the library to send them to me?
- Are there resources that I need to learn how to use, such as a CD-ROM that has to work on my computer or a course Web site that I need to access using a username and password?
- Do I know how to contact the administration office and where to submit assignments?
- Is there a compulsory residential camp or a voluntary one? If I am going to attend a camp, what accommodations and travel do I need to organize?

During a Course

A good start to a course is important. However, you also need to keep working, making sure you study the course materials, complete assignments, and prepare for the examination. Ask the following questions regularly during the course:

- Am I keeping to my study schedule?
- When is the next assignment due?
- Am I understanding the course content?

- When and how am I going to ask the teacher about the content I am having difficulty understanding? I must not hesitate to contact the teacher.
- Am I contributing enough to course Internet discussion forums? Reading the teacher's postings and those of other students is useful, but I should also post messages so that I can help others and they can help me.
- Am I attempting the self-exercises? I need to remember that doing exercises is a better test of my understanding than only reading the questions and looking at the answers.
- Am I making notes while using the learning resources? I must remember that writing notes and highlighting course materials can help me understand.
- Am I ready for the next on-campus class? Do I have questions for the teacher and my visit to the library planned?

The Learning Contract—Your Expectations of the Teacher and the Teacher's Expectations of You

Flexible learning is more like a service than a physical and tangible product. The output, that is, your understanding of course concepts, is coproduced by yourself, the teacher, and other students.

As a student, you can expect the following from the teacher:

- Where possible, concepts will be related to your environment. For example, in a business course the teacher can refer to local businesses. Even if the teacher is in a different country, efforts should be made to relate concepts to your everyday life.
- You should have an awareness of what the teacher thinks about the merits of particular concepts and arguments. That is, as well as resources produced by other experts, there should also be resources, such as notes and a course Web site, written and maintained by the teacher.
- Any information about assignments and examination questions discussed in optional on-campus classes will be sent to you if you choose not to attend.
- The communications channels such as the phone, e-mail, and visiting the teacher's office will be open. If the teacher is going

to be out of contact for more than three workdays, you have a right to know this before it happens.

- At the start of the course, the extent to which the teacher plans to contribute to any Internet-based discussion groups is explained.
- At the start of the course, you will be told how quickly the teacher aims to respond to e-mails.
- Assignments will be assessed and returned according to institutional guidelines. If you are not sure of the guidelines and the teacher has not indicated how quickly your work will be returned, contact the teacher or the administration office.

The course teacher can expect the following from you and your fellow students:

- You will be committed to your study schedule.
- If you have difficulties adapting to flexible learning and developing the necessary study skills, you will contact the teacher, the institution's student support services, or both as soon as possible.
- You will contact the teacher, other students, or both when you have difficulties understanding the course content. It is important that you do not delay seeking assistance.
- Even if you have no difficulties, you will contact the teacher at least once. Doing so is polite and offers an ideal way of establishing a professional relationship.
- Any communication the teacher sends, such as a letter or an e-mail, will be carefully read and acted upon. For example, saying that you were not aware of the change to the date of an on-campus class is not a valid excuse when it was explained in the last two weekly e-mails sent by the teacher.
- You accept that you are not the only student in the course and that the teacher most likely also has responsibilities for other courses, as well as research and administrative duties. Therefore, you understand that the teacher will not instantly reply to your questions.
- The teacher will "hear" your voice, your views, and your analyses through your assignments and contributions to Internet-based discussions.

- You will acknowledge all sources of information used in assignments. To do otherwise is a breach of the trust between you and the teacher.

Making the Most of On-Campus Classes

In many flexible learning courses, you have no face-to-face contact with the teacher and other students. However, some do include a combination of compulsory and optional on-campus classes. Here are some guidelines to help you make the most of any such occasions:

- In the weeks leading to an on-campus class, write down questions you want to ask the teacher.
- Aim to be up-to-date with your study schedule. The more you have studied the course notes, the better prepared you will be to use the valuable face-to-face time to ask about concepts you are having difficulty understanding.
- Participate in discussions and group activities. Be proactive. Although e-mail and Internet-based forums are useful tools, nothing is as effective and efficient as talking to people face-to-face. The relationships you form can help you throughout the course and beyond.
- Make the most of your time on-campus. Classes usually do not take the whole day. So use the remaining time to visit the library to find information for assignments. Visit the student support services if you feel the need to further develop your flexible learning skills.

TOPIC 11.4: MAKING THE MOST OF LEARNING RESOURCES

In this topic, some strategies for using print-based packages and course Web sites are described. Although the focus is on these two common types of flexible learning resources, you are likely to use many others, such as teachers, fellow students, videotapes, CD-ROMs, the World Wide Web, newspapers, journals, and libraries. It is important to use a variety of resources to help you understand a course. Some will be essential (these are called core resources), while others will be supplementary and will help you with particular parts of a course.

As you use a resource, keep asking yourself the following questions about the resource and the course content:

- Why am I using this resource?
- Where am I?
- Where can I go?
- What have I seen?
- How does this relate to my world?
- How can I determine if I understand?
- What do other people think?

The following strategies for using print-based packages and course Web sites are based on what I have seen successful students doing. They can provide a foundation upon which you build your study practices. I recommend that you contact the teacher for additional advice tailored to the course you are studying.

Using Print-Based Packages

A print-based package consists of course notes specially designed for flexible learning environments. The course teacher or other teachers within the institution usually write the package. Use the following strategies and advice to maximize the usefulness of such notes.

Use the Learning Objectives

A package will include course objectives and, if it is large enough to be divided into units, it should also have unit objectives. Before starting a unit, read each objective and self-evaluate your ability to achieve it. Ask yourself, "Can I achieve this objective?" Your answer will help you decide the extent to which you need to study the related notes. Once you have studied the notes, ask the question again. In this way, you use the learning objectives to help focus your study.

Self-Exercises Are Valuable, Especially When Attempted Before Looking at the Answers

A self-exercise is a question or task and a response that consists of an answer and ideally an explanation. They are designed to help you self-evaluate your understanding of course content. Exactly how and when you attempt such exercises is your decision. For example, you could attempt each exercise as you come across it in the course notes or wait until you have studied an entire unit, and then attempt all unit exercises. What is important is that you make a good attempt at answering an exercise before you look at the response. Resist the temptation to read the question, look at the answer, and tell yourself, "Oh yes, I would have answered the question correctly."

Relate the Notes to Your Environment

As you read course notes, ask yourself, "How does this relate to where I live?" and "What are local examples that will help me understand?" Packages will often include activities that help you answer these questions. For example, to understand the theory of queuing, as it applies in the hospitality industry, it may be recommended that you watch people ordering lunchtime meals at a local fast-food business. It can be tempting to only read such suggestions. But remember that teachers make such a recommendation because they believe it will help you understand the course.

Discuss the Package with the Teacher and Other Students

Maximize your communications with the teacher and other students to help you develop your understanding. For example, if there are concepts you do not adequately understand, contact people through methods such as e-mail, a Web forum, the phone, or meeting them face-to-face.

Study Course Readings

Course readings are items such as journal articles and magazine and newspaper extracts that have been included in a package. Teachers decide to make an article a course reading only after careful thought, as in most situations the institution pays a reproduction fee to the copyright holder. Readings written for an academic audience can be difficult to understand. But if a teacher has considered an article important enough to include in a package, you must study it. Often journal articles are valuable tools for helping you develop an understanding of the contrasting views of experts and provide perspectives different from the teacher's.

Highlight Notes and Make Notes

A well-designed package will leave room for you to write directly on the pages. Do not hesitate to do this. Often jotting down notes helps you understand the concepts and provides useful reminders when studying for the examination. At the end of a course, your package should look well used, full of highlighted sections and handwritten notes.

Using Course Web Sites

A course Web site is maintained by the teacher and can be used as

- a source of course notes;
- a frequently asked questions (FAQs) database;
- a computer-mediated contact environment in which you communicate with other students and the teacher; and
- a method of distributing information that previously was distributed on paper.

Many of the strategies applicable to using print-based packages also apply to course Web sites. In addition, the following strategies and advice can help in maximizing their usefulness.

Organize Adequate Internet Access

As soon as possible, and preferably before the course starts, find out what a course Web site will be used for and think about whether your access to the Internet is sufficient. For example, if a site will be mainly used to provide a discussion forum, then weekly access from an Internet café could be sufficient. However, if a site will be a core resource where the majority of course notes will be provided, you may need regular and fast Internet access from your home.

Regularly Check a Course Web Site

Check a course Web site at least once a week. A teacher will often post announcements such as changes to on-campus classes, days the teacher will be out of contact, and corrections and additions to notes.

If the Web Site Contains Pages That Will Not Change During the Course, Then Consider Downloading Them to Your Computer

It can be more convenient to use notes stored on your computer than to have to regularly spend time connected to the Internet. Sometimes a teacher will place course notes on a Web site. For example, the notes for an entire course may be available from week 1. After checking with the teacher to ensure that the notes will not change and that you are allowed to copy them, consider downloading the notes. The extent to which this is possible depends on the types of activities on the Web pages. For example, some activities that involve interacting with simulations cannot be downloaded from a Web server.

To Print or Not to Print?

Before printing out a Web page ask yourself, "Does this page contain information important enough for me to have a copy?" If the answer is yes, then ask yourself, "Will a copy on my computer be sufficient?" If the answer is yes, then download a copy. Otherwise go ahead and print the Web page. Reading from a computer screen is not always easy and convenient and therefore it is tempting to print out a copy of every page. However, first ask yourself the questions.

Contribute to Discussion Forums

An Internet-based discussion forum is used for communicating with the teacher and other students. Although the actions of the teacher play a key role in determining the roles of a discussion forum, you also need to take responsibility for maintaining it. If you have a question or something you want to debate, post a message to the course forum. When posting a message, keep in mind the following guidelines that can help in creating and maintaining an effective forum:

- Use a subject heading when you post a message. This heading helps your fellow students and the teacher follow the discussion. Do not use someone else's subject heading when you want to introduce a new topic.
- When replying to a message, include only the parts of the original message you are replying to. Especially resist quoting someone quoting someone else. Such messages are frustrating to read and most likely will be ignored.
- Remember, the longer the message, the harder it is to read, the more tedious it becomes, and the more likely it will be ignored.
- Use upper and lowercase text. Messages in all capital letters are the equivalent of shouting.
- Remember that everyone studies at a different rate. Therefore, be tolerant of people posting messages about topics that you have finished studying. Use your understanding to help your fellow students.
- Be diplomatic. Criticism is always harsher when written. Read your message to yourself before you send it. So often we regret messages we send when we are angry, tired, busy, or feel strongly about something.
- Stay calm. Remember, not everyone's computer skills are the same as yours, and everyone's language skills are different.

KEY POINTS

1. Many of the study skills that apply to fully on-campus courses also work in flexible learning courses.
2. The ability to question oneself and others is important when studying a flexible learning course. This helps in maintaining a study schedule and developing an understanding of course content.
3. A student should make the most of any opportunities to communicate with the teacher and other students. A student needs to be proactive and speak out.

References

Atkins, M. J. (1993). Evaluating interactive technologies for learning. *Journal of Curriculum Studies,* 25, 333-342.

Bell, M., Bush, D., Nicholson, P., O'Brien, D., and Tran, T. (2002). *Universities Online: A Survey of Online Education and Services in Australia.* Canberra, Australia: Commonwealth Department of Education Science and Training, 02-A Occasional Paper Services, Higher Education Group.

Bodner, G. M. (1986). Constructivism: A theory of knowledge. *Journal of Chemical Education,* 63(10), 873-878.

Collis, B. and Moonen, J. (2001). *Flexible Learning in a Digital World.* London: Kogan Page.

Costa, A. L. and Kallick, B. (1993). Through the lens of a critical friend. *Educational Leadership,* 51(2), 49-51.

Cunningham, D. L. (1991). Assessing constructions and constructing assessments: A dialogue. *Educational Technology,* 31(5), 13-17.

Downes, S. (2003). Copyright, ethics and theft. <http://www.downes.ca>.

Dunkin, M. J. (1987). Introduction to section 4: Classroom processes. In M. J. Dunkin (Ed.), *The International Encyclopaedia of Teaching and Teacher Education* (pp. 313-326). Oxford, Great Britain: Pergamon Press.

Feenberg, A. (1989). The written word. In R. D. Mason and A. R. Kay (Eds.), *Mindweave, Communication, Computers and Distance Education.* Oxford, Great Britain: Pergamon Press.

Gall, J. E. and Hannafin, M. J. (1994). A framework for the study of hypertext. *Instructional Science,* 22, 207-232.

Hammond, N. and Allinson, L. (1988). Development and evaluation of a CAL system for non-formal domains: The hitch-hiker's guide to cognition. *Computers and Education,* 12, 215-220.

Hotel and Tourism Management (HTM). (2000). *Definitive Programme Document for the Bachelor of Arts (Honors) in Hotel and Catering Management (Part-Time) Programme of Study.* Hong Kong: School of Hotel and Tourism Management, The Hong Kong Polytechnic University.

Jonassen, D. H. (1991). Objectivism versus constructivism: Do we need a new philosophical paradigm? *Educational Technology Research and Development,* 39(3), 5-14.

Jonassen, D. H., Wilson, B. G., Wang, S., and Grabinger, R. S. (1993). Constructivist uses of expert systems to support learning. *Journal of Computer-Based Instruction,* 20, 86-94.

Laurillard, D. (1993). *Rethinking University Teaching*. London: Routledge.

Levinson, P. (1999). *Digital McLuhan*. London: Routledge.

Macquarie Library. (1998). *The Macquarie Concise Dictionary* (Third Edition). Australia: The Macquarie Library.

Mitchell, I. (1993). Teaching for quality learning. Unpublished doctoral dissertation. Monash University, Melbourne, Australia.

Postman, N. (1987). *Amusing Ourselves to Death*. London: Methuen London.

Race, P. (1993). *The Open Learning Handbook* (Second Edition). London: Kogan Page.

Ross, S. M. and Morrison, G. R. (1989). In search of a happy medium in instructional technology research: Issues concerning external validity, media replications, and learner control, *Educational Technology Research and Development,* 37(1), 19-33.

Rowntree, D. (1995). Teaching and learning online: A correspondence education for the 21st century? *British Journal of Educational Technology,* 26(3), 205-215.

Strike, K. A. and Posner, G. J. (1985). A conceptual change view of learning and understanding. In L. H. T. West and A. L. Pines (Eds.), *Cognitive Structure and Conceptual Change* (pp. 211-231). New York: Academic Press.

Viau, R. and Larivée, J. (1993). Learning tools with hypertext: An experiment. *Computers and Education,* 20, 11-16.

von Glasersfeld, E. (1984). An introduction to radical constructivism. In P. Watzlawick (Ed.), *The Invented Reality: How Do We Know What We Believe We Know? (Contributions to Constructivism)* (pp. 17-40). New York: W. W. Norton.

von Glasersfeld, E. (1990). An exposition of constructivism: Why some like it radical. In R. B. Davis, C. A. Maher, and N. Noddings (Eds.), *Constructivist Views on the Teaching and Learning of Mathematics* (pp. 19-29). Journal for Research in Mathematics Education, Monograph No. 4. Reston, VA: The National Council of Teachers of Mathematics.

Wheatley, G. H. (1989). Constructivist perspectives on science and mathematics learning. Paper presented at the First International Conference on the History and Philosophy of Science in Science Teaching, Tallahassee, Florida.

White, R. T. (1988). *Learning Science*. Oxford, Great Britain: Basil Blackwell.

Williams, G. (1997). Computer mediated communication. <http://www.csu.edu.au/division/celt/edtech/CMC/cmc.htm>.

Williams, G. (2001). Learning at a distance. *Journal of Teaching in Travel and Tourism,* 1(1), 109-119.

Williams, G. (2003). Implementation of a course management system: Experiences and students' thoughts. *Journal of Teaching in Travel and Tourism,* 3(2), 59-69.

Williams, G. and McKercher, B. (1999). The Internet and tourism education. In V. C. S. Heung, J. Ap, and K. K. F. Wong (Eds.), *Tourism 2000 Asia Pacific's Role in the New Millennium: Proceedings of the Asia Pacific Tourism Association Fifth Annual Conference* (pp. 883-890). Hong Kong: The Hong Kong Polytechnic University.

Winn, W. D. (1991). The assumptions of constructivism and instructional design. *Educational Technology,* 31(9), 38-40.

Wittrock, M. C. (1985). Learning science by generating new conceptions from old ideas. In L. H. T. West and A. L. Pines (Eds.), *Cognitive Structure and Conceptual Change* (pp. 259-266). New York: Academic Press.

Index

Page numbers followed by the letter "b" indicate boxed material; those followed by the letter "t" indicate tables; and those followed by the letter "f" indicate figures.

Access, Web site, 147-148
Adaptation, and reproduction
    permission, 77
Advanced organizer, 153
    minutes, 20, 22
Advertising, Web site access, 146-147
Attribution license, 76
Audio, in course Web sites, 157, 158

Brainstorming, 173

Chatter, CMC environment, 178
Computer-mediated contact (CMC)
    advantages, 168-169
    challenges, 169
    contributing to, 180, 233-234
    definition, 165
    guidance document, 61t-63t
    managerial strategies, 179-181
    moderation, 172
    social strategies, 177-179
    student training/support, 183-184
    teacher training/support, 181-183
    teaching strategies, 173-176
    types, 167
Constructivism, 53, 54-55
    students' roles, 56-57
    teachers' roles, 57-58
Content elements
    definition, 135
    development, 140-144
    storyboards, 143f

Content writer
    contextualization, 68, 69
    course outline, 116
    definition, 35
    and guidance document, 60
    and quality content, 59
    recognition, 44
    rewards of, 50-51
    role, 35-36
    syllabus understanding, 87
    teachers as, 50b
    unit drafting, 113
Contextualization, 68
Copyright
    definition, 75
    enforcement, 80-81
    and flexible learning notes, 99
    identifying print items, 110-111
    identifying Web items, 139-140
    ownership, 79
    use of material, 75-76
Core learning resource, 5
Course content
    communication, 72
    contextualization, 68
    media selection, 59, 89
    understanding, 70-72
Course management system (CMS), 185
    advantages, 187, 190
    challenges, 189, 190-191
    definition, 186
    training and support, 198-201
Course outline, writing, 73-74, 116, 146
Course syllabus, 58, 87

Deadlines, 25-26
Design
  balance, 65
  contextualization, 68
  definition, 13
  guidance document, 60-64
  media-dependent aspects, 13
  media-independent aspects, 13
  print resources, 117-123
  Web-based resources, 148-161
Design specification, 117
Discussion points, 122, 123, 156
Distance learning, versus flexible
    learning as term, 4
Drafting, print resources, 112-113

Educational designer
  contextualization, 68, 69
  course outline, 116
  course syllabus, 87
  definition, 36
  role, 36-37
  unit drafting, 113
Element, definition, 135
E-mail, 167
  teacher's weekly, 210-211, 212f
Evaluation, definition, 13
Experts' views, 122-123

Facilitation, meetings, 22
Fair-use principles, 76
"Final" date setting, 26
Flexible learning
  and computer-mediated contact, 167
  and constructivism, 58
  copyrighting, 79-81
  course outline importance, 73
  definition, 3, 14
  development model, 12f
  educational designer
      responsibilities, 214
  environment, 2, 14
  learning contract, 227-228

Flexible learning *(continued)*
  media choice, 84
  notes, 99
  on-campus classes, 212-213, 229
  and print resources, 97
  project beginnings, 28-29
  project management, 16-22
  project team, 31-44, 38t
  student advantages, 220-221
  student challenges, 222-224
  teacher introduction, 207-209
  teacher maintenance, 209-213
  teacher preparation, 205-206
  terminology, 2
  use strategies, 229-234
  versus distance learning as term, 4
  and Web sites, 135

General educational design guidelines,
    123-124
"Genryoko Sushi—Competitive
    Advantage," example, 120-121
Guidance document, 60, 110
  HTM project, 64b
  sample extract, 61t-63t
  writing guidelines, 64
Guidelines
  CMC contributions, 180
  CMC teaching strategies, 173-176
  design, 65-72
  educational designer, 123-124
  guidance document writing, 64
  netiquette, 180
  print style, 124-125
  student training
      in CMC use, 183-184
      in CMS, 200-201
  teacher training
      in CMC use, 182-183
      in CMS, 198-200
  Web design, 160-161

Header
    print, 118,
    Web page, 154
Highlighted box, 153, 156
Home page, 141f, 154
Hong Kong Polytechnic University,
        School of HTM, 7
Hotel and Tourism Management
        (HTM) project, 4
    case study, 7-11
    CMC teaching strategies, 176b-177b
    compulsory class, 208b
    content elements, 143f
    content writers, 50b
    contextualization, 69b
    course management system,
        188b-189b, 193b
    development model, 11-14
    educational designer support, 215b
    e-mail access, 86b
    guidance document, 64b
    home page, 150f
    lecture pack, 100b
    media variety, 96b
    orientation, 207b
    print package development
        timetable, 111b
    print packaging, 115b
    project beginnings, 29-31
    project ownership, 47b
    project team, 34b
    resource development and buying,
        32b
    stakeholder meeting, 42-44
    storyboards, 142f
    timeline, 9, 10t
    unit reviewing, 114b
    Web page, 141f, 151f
    Web site characteristics, 136b
    Web site development, 133b
    Web site shell, 141b
How Can I Determine If I Understand?,
        155-156
    design, 54, 70-72
    print, 122

How Does This Relate to My World?,
        design, 54, 68-70
    print, 120-122
    Web site, 155

"Implementation at Chek Lap Kok
        Airport," example, 121
Index
    print, 118
    Web page, 155
Industry practitioners, video interviews,
        159-160
Institution
    course management system (CMS),
        191-192, 194-195
    definition, 7
    media selection, 91-92
    print resource advantages, 102
Integrating media, 95b
Interactivity, Web sites, 152-153
Internet, definition, 130
Intranet, definition, 130

Lateness, at meetings, 21
Learning contract, 227-229
Learning resources
    definition, 2
    design guidelines, 65-72
    as media, 84
    project beginnings, 29-31
    source variety, 31
Lecture notes, 99
Link rot, 135
Links, 156, 157, 162
Listserv, 167

Maintenance
    definition, 13, 14
    print resources, 126-127
    Web-based resources, 161-162
Media
    and course content, 92-93
    electronic. *See* Web-based resources

Media *(continued)*
    in flexible learning, 84
    institutional factors, 91-92
    print. *See* Print-based resources
    students needs, 87-90
    teachers needs, 90-91
    variety, 94-95
Media-dependent aspects, design, 13
Media-independent aspects, design, 13,
        53
Medium, definition, 84
Meetings
    after strategies, 21-22
    before strategies, 20
    during strategies, 21
    effectiveness, 19
Minutes, meeting, 21, 22

Navigation elements, definition, 135
Navigational buttons, 154
Netiquette guidelines, 180
No derivative works license, 76
Noncommercial license, 76

Objective checklist, 122
On-campus classes, 212-213, 229
Online polling, 175
Orientation, first-year students, 206-207

Packaging
    deciding, 113-114
    definition, 113
    elements, 115b
Pedagogy, 90
Posting, reworking, 175
Predevelopment considerations, 30-31
Predict-observe-explain simulations,
        156
Prepurchase considerations, 30
Print production
    content finalized, 114-116
    course outline, 116

Print production *(continued)*
    design, 117-125
    duplication, 116-117
    first draft, 112
    maintenance, 126-127
    process stages, 105, 106f
    project team meetings, 107-108
    review, 112
    revision, 127-128
Print resources
    advantages, 101, 102
    definition, 98
    developing, 102-104
    disadvantages, 101
    financial costs, 103-104
    production, 104-117
    students' use strategies, 230-232
    style guidelines, 124-125
Print-based resources, 68, 70, 97
Production
    definition, 13
    print resources, 104-117
    Web-based resources, 135-161
Project development, versus purchase,
        30
Project management
    aids, 22-23
    as organized chaos, 24-26
    software, 23-24
Project manager
    characteristics, 17-18
    CMS training and support, 197-201
    course outline writing, 116
    definition, 16
    effective meetings, 19-22
    media selection, 85
    senior staff support, 18-19
    team, 33
    unit drafting, 113
    Web site production, 144
Project ownership, 44-45
Project team
    content writer, 35-36
    definition, 33
    educational designer, 36-37
    formation, 32

Project team *(continued)*
   other members, 33, 38t
   print production, 107
   project manager, 33, 34
   Web site production, 138
Prototype site, 142
   evaluation, 143-144

Quality content, 12, 59, 60f, 139

Real-life simulation, 158
Reproduction permission, 75, 76
   obtaining, 77-79, 78f
Return on investment, 4-7
Revision
   definition, 13, 14
   print resources, 127-128
   Web-based resources, 162-163
Rudeness, CMC environment, 178

School, definition, 18
Self-exercises, 71, 72, 122
Semester, definition, 205
"Something to think about" section,
   120-121
Stakeholder, definition, 37
Stakeholder meetings, 37-38
   goal of, 39
   HTM project, 42-44
   issues to discuss, 40-41
   management strategies, 41-42
   program flexibility decisions, 46t
Storyboards, Web site development,
   140, 142f
"Strategic Management Process"
   content elements, 143f
   example, 119
   home page, 150f
   storyboard, 142f
   Web page, 141f, 151f

Students
   assessment opportunities, 70-72
   CMC training, 183-184
   CMS
      advantages, 187-188
      challenges, 189
      training, 200-201
   communication, 72
   contextualization, 68-70
   determining needs of, 87-88
   flexible learning
      advantages, 220-221
      challenges, 222-224
      course maintenance, 224-227
      course orientation, 206-207
   learning contract, 227-229
   on-campus classes, 229
   print resource advantages, 102
   print-based package use, 230-232
   resource use, 65-67
   technology access, 88-90
   Web site course use, 232-234
Supplementary learning resource, 5
Supporting resource, 2, 3

Table of contents, 118
Teachers
   CMC training, 181-183
   CMS
      advantages, 190
      challenges, 190-191
      training, 198-200
      use, 195-197
   and flexible learning, 85-86
      course beginnings, 207-209
      course maintenance, 209-210
      course preparation, 205-206
   as forum moderator, 172
   introduction video, 159
   media selection, 90-91
   on-campus classes, 212-213
   print resource advantages, 102-103
   program participation, 45, 47
   program rewards, 49-51

Teachers *(continued)*
    self-appraisal, 47-49
    weekly e-mail, 210-211, 212f
Teaching
    CMC strategies, 173-176
    in flexible learning environment,
        204
Teaching resource, 2
Technology
    definition, 84
    literacy, 90
    and Web site design, 152
Textbook integration, 123
Timetable
    content element development
        tracking, 145f
    development, 43
    flexibility, 25b
    print package, 108t-110t
    Web pages, 138

Unit, definition, 105
Unit learning objectives, 66
Unit outline, 118
Universal resource locators (URLs),
    179

Video, in course Web sites, 157, 158,
    159-160

Web forum, 167
    contributing, 233-234
Web site
    definition, 130
    elements, 149-152
    hits, 197
    pages, 150f, 151f
    references, 123, 134

Web site production
    content elements, 140-142
    course outline, 146
    design, 148-161
    finalization, 144
    first draft development timetable,
        138-139
    maintenance, 162
    pages, 144
    process stages, 136, 137f
    project team meetings, 138
    prototype, 142-144
    quality content development, 139
    release, 146
    revision, 162-163
    shell development, 140
    testing, 144, 146
Web-based resources, 68, 70, 129
    developing, 131-132
    financial costs, 132-133
    production, 135-161
    students' use strategies, 232-234
    use, 130-131
What Do Other People Think?
    design, 54, 72
    print, 122-123
    Web site, 156-157
Where Am I? Where Can I Go? What
        Have I Seen?
    design, 53, 67-68
    print, 118-119
    Web site, 153-155
Why Am I Using This Resource?
    design, 53, 65-67
    print, 118
    Web site, 153
World Wide Web, 134-135, 167
    addresses, 179
Writing
    course outline, 73-74, 116, 146
    objectives, 66-67

THE HAWORTH HOSPITALITY PRESS®
Hospitality, Travel, and Tourism
K. S. Chon, PhD, Editor in Chief

COMMUNITY DESTINATION MANAGEMENT IN DEVELOPING ECONO-MIES edited by Walter Jamieson. (2006).

MANAGING SUSTAINABLE TOURISM: A LEGACY FOR THE FUTURE by David L. Edgell Sr. (2006).

CASINO INDSUTRY IN ASIA-PACIFIC: DEVELOPMENT, OPERATION, AND IMPACT edited by Cathy H.C. Hsu. (2006).

THE GROWTH STRATEGIES OF HOTEL CHAINS: BEST BUSINESS PRAC-TICES BY LEADING COMPANIES by Onofre Martorell Cunill. (2005).

HANDBOOK FOR DISTANCE LEARNING IN TOURISM by Gary Williams. (2005). "This is an important book for a variety of audiences. As a resource for educational designers (and their managers) in particular, it is invaluable. The book is easy to read, and is full of practical information that can be logically applied in the design and development of flexible learning resources." *Louise Berg, MA, DipED, Lecturer in Education, Charles Sturt University, Australia*

VIETNAM TOURISM by Arthur Asa Berger. (2005). "Fresh and innovative.... Drawing upon Professor Berger's background and experience in cultural studies, this book offers an imaginative and personal portrayal of Vietnam as a tourism destination.... A very welcome addition to the field of destination studies." *Professor Brian King, PhD, Head, School of Hospitality, Tourism & Marketing, Victoria University, Australia*

TOURISM AND HOTEL DEVELOPMENT IN CHINA: FROM POLITICAL TO ECONOMIC SUCCESS by Hanqin Qiu Zhang, Ray Pine, and Terry Lam. (2005). "This is one of the most comprehensive books on China tourism and hotel development. It is one of the best textbooks for educators, students, practitioners, and investors who are interested in china tourism and hotel industry. Readers will experience vast, diversified, and past and current issues that affect every educator, student, practitioner, and investor in China tourism and hotel globally in an instant." *Hailin Qu, PhD, Full Professor and William E. Davis Distinguished Chair, School of Hotel & Restaurant Administration, Oklahoma State University*

THE TOURISM AND LEISURE INDUSTRY: SHAPING THE FUTURE edited by Klaus Weiermair and Christine Mathies. (2004). "If you need or want to know about the impact of globalization, the impact of technology, societal forces of change, the experience economy, adaptive technologies, environmental changes, or the new trend of slow tourism, you need this book. *The Tourism and Leisure Industry* contains a great mix of research and practical information." *Charles R. Goeldner, PhD, Professor Emeritus of Marketing and Tourism, Leeds School of Business, University of Colorado*

OCEAN TRAVEL AND CRUISING: A CULTURAL ANALYSIS by Arthur Asa Berger. (2004). "Dr. Berger presents an interdisciplinary discussion of the cruise industry for the thinking person. This is an enjoyable social psychology travel guide with a little business management thrown in. A great book for the curious to read a week before embarking on a first cruise or for the frequent cruiser to gain a broader insight into exactly what a cruise experience represents." *Carl Braunlich, DBA, Associate Professor, Department of Hospitality and Tourism Management, Purdue University, West Lafayette, Indiana*

STANDING THE HEAT: ENSURING CURRICULUM QUALITY IN CULINARY ARTS AND GASTRONOMY by Joseph A. Hegarty. (2003). "This text provides the genesis of a well-researched, thoughtful, rigorous, and sound theoretical framework for the enlargement and expansion of higher education programs in culinary arts and gastronomy." *John M. Antun, PhD, Founding Director, National Restaurant Institute, School of Hotel, Restaurant, and Tourism Management, University of South Carolina*

SEX AND TOURISM: JOURNEYS OF ROMANCE, LOVE, AND LUST edited by Thomas G. Bauer and Bob McKercher. (2003). "Anyone interested in or concerned about the impact of tourism on society and particularly in the developing world, should read this book. It explores a subject that has long remained ignored, almost a taboo area for many governments, institutions, and organizations. It demonstrates that the stereotyping of 'sex tourism' is too simple and travel and sex have many manifestations. The book follows its theme in an innovative and original way." *Carson L. Jenkins, PhD, Professor of International Tourism, University of Strathclyde, Glasgow, Scotland*

CONVENTION TOURISM: INTERNATIONAL RESEARCH AND INDUSTRY PERSPECTIVES edited by Karin Weber and Kye-Sung Chon. (2002). "This comprehensive book is truly global in its perspective. The text points out areas of needed research—a great starting point for graduate students, university faculty, and industry professionals alike. While the focus is mainly academic, there is a lot of meat for this burgeoning industry to chew on as well." *Patti J. Shock, CPCE, Professor and Department Chair, Tourism and Convention Administration, Harrah College of Hotel Administration, University of Nevada–Las Vegas*

CULTURAL TOURISM: THE PARTNERSHIP BETWEEN TOURISM AND CULTURAL HERITAGE MANAGEMENT by Bob McKercher and Hilary du Cros. (2002). "The book brings together concepts, perspectives, and practicalities that must be understood by both cultural heritage and tourism managers, and as such is a must-read for both." *Hisashi B. Sugaya, AICP, Former Chair, International Council of Monuments and Sites, International Scientific Committee on Cultural Tourism; Former Executive Director, Pacific Asia Travel Association Foundation, San Francisco, CA*

TOURISM IN THE ANTARCTIC: OPPORTUNITIES, CONSTRAINTS, AND FUTURE PROSPECTS by Thomas G. Bauer. (2001). "Thomas Bauer presents a wealth of detailed information on the challenges and opportunities facing tourism operators in this last great tourism frontier." *David Mercer, PhD, Associate Professor, School of Geography & Environmental Science, Monash University, Melbourne, Australia*

SERVICE QUALITY MANAGEMENT IN HOSPITALITY, TOURISM, AND LEISURE edited by Jay Kandampully, Connie Mok, and Beverley Sparks. (2001). "A must-read. . . . a treasure. . . . pulls together the work of scholars across the globe, giving you access to new ideas, international research, and industry examples from around the world." *John Bowen, Professor and Director of Graduate Studies, William F. Harrah College of Hotel Administration, University of Nevada, Las Vegas*

TOURISM IN SOUTHEAST ASIA: A NEW DIRECTION edited by K. S. (Kaye) Chon. (2000). "Presents a wide array of very topical discussions on the specific challenges facing the tourism industry in Southeast Asia. A great resource for both scholars and practitioners." *Dr. Hubert B. Van Hoof, Assistant Dean/Associate Professor, School of Hotel and Restaurant Management, Northern Arizona University*

THE PRACTICE OF GRADUATE RESEARCH IN HOSPITALITY AND TOURISM edited by K. S. Chon. (1999). "An excellent reference source for students pursuing graduate degrees in hospitality and tourism." *Connie Mok, PhD, CHE, Associate Professor, Conrad N. Hilton College of Hotel and Restaurant Management, University of Houston, Texas*

THE INTERNATIONAL HOSPITALITY MANAGEMENT BUSINESS: MANAGEMENT AND OPERATIONS by Larry Yu. (1999). "The abundant real-world examples and cases provided in the text enable readers to understand the most up-to-date developments in international hospitality business." *Zheng Gu, PhD, Associate Professor, College of Hotel Administration, University of Nevada, Las Vegas*

CONSUMER BEHAVIOR IN TRAVEL AND TOURISM by Abraham Pizam and Yoel Mansfeld. (1999). "A must for anyone who wants to take advantage of new global opportunities in this growing industry." *Bonnie J. Knutson, PhD, School of Hospitality Business, Michigan State University*

LEGALIZED CASINO GAMING IN THE UNITED STATES: THE ECONOMIC AND SOCIAL IMPACT edited by Cathy H. C. Hsu. (1999). "Brings a fresh new look at one of the areas in tourism that has not yet received careful and serious consideration in the past." *Muzaffer Uysal, PhD, Professor of Tourism Research, Virginia Polytechnic Institute and State University, Blacksburg*

HOSPITALITY MANAGEMENT EDUCATION edited by Clayton W. Barrows and Robert H. Bosselman. (1999). "Takes the mystery out of how hospitality management education programs function and serves as an excellent resource for individuals interested in pursuing the field." *Joe Perdue, CCM, CHE, Director, Executive Masters Program, College of Hotel Administration, University of Nevada, Las Vegas*

MARKETING YOUR CITY, U.S.A.: A GUIDE TO DEVELOPING A STRATEGIC TOURISM MARKETING PLAN by Ronald A. Nykiel and Elizabeth Jascolt. (1998). "An excellent guide for anyone involved in the planning and marketing of cities and regions. . . . A terrific job of synthesizing an otherwise complex procedure." *James C. Maken, PhD, Associate Professor, Babcock Graduate School of Management, Wake Forest University, Winston-Salem, North Carolina*

Order a copy of this book with this form or online at:
http://www.haworthpress.com/store/product.asp?sku=5346

HANDBOOK FOR DISTANCE LEARNING IN TOURISM

_____in hardbound at $49.95 (ISBN-13: 978-0-7890-1859-5; ISBN-10: 0-7890-1859-4)

_____in softbound at $34.95 (ISBN-13: 978-0-7890-1860-1; ISBN-10: 0-7890-1860-8)

Or order online and use special offer code HEC25 in the shopping cart.

COST OF BOOKS_____

POSTAGE & HANDLING_____
*(US: $4.00 for first book & $1.50
for each additional book)*
*(Outside US: $5.00 for first book
& $2.00 for each additional book)*

SUBTOTAL_____

IN CANADA: ADD 7% GST_____

STATE TAX_____
*(NJ, NY, OH, MN, CA, IL, IN, PA, & SD
residents, add appropriate local sales tax)*

FINAL TOTAL_____
*(If paying in Canadian funds,
convert using the current
exchange rate, UNESCO
coupons welcome)*

☐ **BILL ME LATER:** (Bill-me option is good on
US/Canada/Mexico orders only; not good to
jobbers, wholesalers, or subscription agencies.)

☐ Check here if billing address is different from
shipping address and attach purchase order and
billing address information.

Signature_____

☐ **PAYMENT ENCLOSED: $**_____

☐ **PLEASE CHARGE TO MY CREDIT CARD.**

☐ Visa ☐ MasterCard ☐ AmEx ☐ Discover
☐ Diner's Club ☐ Eurocard ☐ JCB

Account # _____

Exp. Date_____

Signature_____

Prices in US dollars and subject to change without notice.

NAME_____

INSTITUTION_____

ADDRESS_____

CITY_____

STATE/ZIP_____

COUNTRY_____ COUNTY (NY residents only)_____

TEL_____ FAX_____

E-MAIL_____

May we use your e-mail address for confirmations and other types of information? ☐ Yes ☐ No
We appreciate receiving your e-mail address and fax number. Haworth would like to e-mail or fax special
discount offers to you, as a preferred customer. **We will never share, rent, or exchange your e-mail address
or fax number.** We regard such actions as an invasion of your privacy.

Order From Your Local Bookstore or Directly From
The Haworth Press, Inc.
10 Alice Street, Binghamton, New York 13904-1580 • USA
TELEPHONE: 1-800-HAWORTH (1-800-429-6784) / Outside US/Canada: (607) 722-5857
FAX: 1-800-895-0582 / Outside US/Canada: (607) 771-0012
E-mail to: orders@haworthpress.com

For orders outside US and Canada, you may wish to order through your local
sales representative, distributor, or bookseller.
For information, see http://haworthpress.com/distributors

(Discounts are available for individual orders in US and Canada only, not booksellers/distributors.)

PLEASE PHOTOCOPY THIS FORM FOR YOUR PERSONAL USE.
http://www.HaworthPress.com   BOF04